INDIGO EDUCATION -

For All Ages!

A MANUAL FOR MENTORING ME -
and YOU?

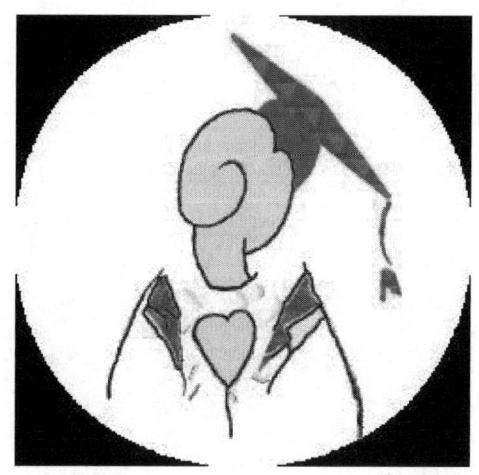

CHRISTOPHER GILMORE

Actor, Author, Teacher, Learner

A foreword by Emeritus Professor Tricia David

ATMA DOVETALES EDUCATIONAL

34 Clifton Avenue

Crewe, Cheshire

CW2 7PZ, UK

07837971408

~

First published in Great Britain in 2016

Typesetting by David Blackhurst

ISBN   9781787230286

AKNOWLEDGEMENTS

Now in my eighties my memories stretch back a long way. So hopefully it is not to too late to thank my parents for rearing, with enough care, their strange, and often very ailing, first-born. Yes, I 'know' I did ask to be born to them!

More recently, after making a living as an actor, the problematic words of education provided my pension. But not without my restless desire to improve what was then known as the chalk face. As a maverick Drama Teacher, I innovated many ways of stimulating the latent creativity in my students. The effect of these ploys was noticed. This is to introduce a list of names who, professionally, allowed my more off-beat approaches to flourish.

Thank you Galina Dolya for inviting me to teach philosophy to 4+-year-olds for a decade of happy lessons. One single parent, Susan Wilmot-Josife encouraged me to set up with her and others like David Renner, INaSENSE. The strain of finding an education system to suit her three very diverse children was the core of my book, FREE SCHOOLS??? - That's the Spirit! (Pegasus/Vanguard Press, 2010.) Although an award-winning writer by then, the book was mostly ignored by traditional educationists.

It was largely due to those two ladies, supported by David Renner, that ATMA Enterprises was formed in May, 2015. The enabling team that follows are featured in these pages and I will thank them one and all until the day I graduate to my next heavenly classroom.

May the Blessings Be

Christopher Gilmore

FOREWORD

Tricia David

Emeritus Professor of Education
at Canterbury Christchurch University

Christopher Gilmore's aim is to bring together his life-work in this enchanting book and I feel very privileged to have been asked to contribute a foreword to his important text. He is one of the most accomplished people I have had the good fortune to know. In this book he tells readers of some of his experiences; his stage acting, teaching and his prolific writing.

All these experiences have helped Christopher synthesize knowledge from a wide variety of fields, to support his passionate belief in the need to nurture the talents of every child and adult. He is distressed by the current climate in Education, where only a narrow range of subjects and achievements is valued.

Christopher is definitely a person who wishes to see a hundred - or even more - flowers bloom. And he tells us in this book that he believes we may each have flowers with which we were not only born but inherited from former lives. While some of us may believe otherwise, thinkers like Christopher are very valuable in making us respectfully think of alternative explanations, while at the same time

agreeing we should cherish and nourish the talents of each child and adult we meet in our work and in our wider lives.

Rightly proud of his successes as an unorthodox teacher, trained but with no university degree, Christopher throws us another challenge - but not all who have not attained a university degree are as gifted as he. We who are or have been Teacher Educators (and this is a title we have struggled to hang onto despite being dubbed Teacher Trainers - Training and Education are different in depth and expectations) do need to return with regularity to examine what we provide for new entrants to the profession and to ask ourselves what difference this makes to the learners our students will encounter, whether children or adults.

Sadly, in recent years, some courses for would-be teachers have become focused on the 'delivery' of the National Curriculum. I remember one mature undergraduate on an Early Childhood Studies degree course asking me how it was that her daughter - also an undergraduate but on a teaching degree - was being expected to prepare lesson plans for a class of children she had yet to meet.

This was at a time when we were struggling to have Early Childhood Studies degrees recognised as suitable qualifications for entry to a Post Graduate Certificate in Education course in order to qualify as teachers. This wise young woman realised that in order to plan learning experiences for children one needs to know the children, their interests, enthusiasms, joys and earlier encounters first, rather than imposing meaningless, irrelevant content or processes on whole groups or classes.

So while I am sad that Christopher seems occasionally overly critical of our hard-pressed teachers, when his targets should be elsewhere, he does make us stop the panicky treadmill to analyse whether there might be another way - another way to convince politicians to listen, to take pressure off teachers and schools, so that children, while still achieving in literacy and numeracy, may love what they learn in school because it is an exciting and joyful place to be - a place where they feel themselves loved too.

~

Latest publication in which Christopher has a chapter is:-

The Routledge International Handbook of Philosophies and Theories of Early Childhood Education and Care. Edited by Tricia David, Kathy Goouch and Sacha Powell Routledge/ Taylor & Francis.

ATMA ENTERPRISES

Community Interest Company

Number *10227175*

We are a Social Enterprise co-creating innovative ways for people of all ages to expand their innate potential through person-centred experiential learning.

FOR SELF-EVALUATION

- Y/OUR REVEILLE?

Each of us is special. Every spirited person aims to make this current life ever more special. But how do we make every tomorrow better than every yesterday if doubts and insecurities nibble away at our Self-esteem?

Yet is it not there, this quest...this nagging need to solve life's mysteries? Don't the simplest of questions ache for answers? Questions like - Why are we here? What is Soul? Why do we dream? Why must we die? Is the book you now hold for real? If so, do I buy into its message?

Perhaps we'd be better off not delving, not yearning. But that's not the human heart at its fruitful best. To probe the real reasons for our existence, what if that is exactly why we are here on earth now - to find out? Yet we juggle with doubts, still struggle to make a difference, to change the world, to dream of hope, never knowing who will hold our hand, touch our hearts. By becoming more useful and beautiful, is that secondary to taking complete responsibility for our good selves first?

But succeed we all will! Those blessed with the Indigo consciousness, no matter how at times uncomfortable, sense they need to stay in charge of their own development. And at all levels of love; spiritual, emotional and physical. With insightful contributions from members of the ATMA Team of Enablers, this book is an open-hearted manual for increased Self-reliance.

Self-Esteem is the Master Key. It can lead more quickly to successful goal-setting by kick-starting incremental growth in Self-Awareness. Let your inner alchemy develop more Self-management skills, by sharing your gifts generously with others. In service to the greatest good, with our varied range of Playshops, we say WELCOME...

You ageless ones who discern

Who serve like Indigos learn

What could be finer

You your best miner

Gems in Light good karmas earn.

~

In every sort of weather

Activating Together

Mentor Achievements

As MINING ME vents

Blessings better than white heather!

Table of Contents

1. FORMATIVE **FUN**DAMENTALS

To our INDIGOS you can't dictate

With kids' Creativity relate

There's no point in cursin'

Each their own person

Ageless consciousness they collate

Before schooling, a cardboard-box can become a cave, a car or a castle. Children's pro-active play is formative and can be seen as diagnostic. By impulsively exploring their own learning styles, they experiment with their potential skill-sets. Learners who enjoy asking who, where and why they are, can happily gain Self-esteem through self-knowledge. After all, 'why' is often a favourite word as their need to learn more is triggered by personal curiosity. So intrigue them with a wide variety of unexpected and multi-sensory stimuli. This suggestion is explored later in more depth in the section describing Early Inklings' Emporium.

Exploring universal themes such as the weather, for all ages, every single topic can become the subject of far-reaching creative discussions; preferably over a family meal prepared by all consumers. After all, the same ingredients of life belong to every one of us. And God-given, a family is a mixed ability learning group. By acknowledging this with people of all ages, whether dubbed Indigos or not, modest wonder and mighty gratitude can be expressed by each unique individual. Where an abundance of love is nurtured, creativity is bound to follow. The best creation is the improvements we make of ourselves. Love links, mind thinks, fear shrinks, Soul knows!

Stay watchful though to sensitive persons who hide an inner sense of their own gifts, and maybe retain the opinions of adults as more important than their own. By allowing all of life's pilgrims to discover and develop their own passions, such core powers can form the transformative foundation of their future usefulness to society. Special interest when so identified, first sparked by curiosity fired by enthusiasm, with encouragement this can quickly grow into expertise.

A child's choices respected and supported in this way can become ever more capable. Each has special needs because every unique each one of them, like us, is indeed special. That is the energy that can drive and improve their future prospects. Still waiting for someone to make you happy; to make you feel special?

Using ATMA's personal surveys called Mining Me, one heart-centred, the other more head-centred, these two profiles shared with a group of peers, any disquiet felt about school experiences past, present or to come can become more understood; and along the stepping-stones of Self-Awareness we provide, grow incrementally into more Self-managed Energy Management.

Better still, when newly honed to provide a skill-set of practical tools it can all aid further advancements. That in brief is the presiding purpose of what we of ATMA Enterprises offer. So a warm welcome to these pages.

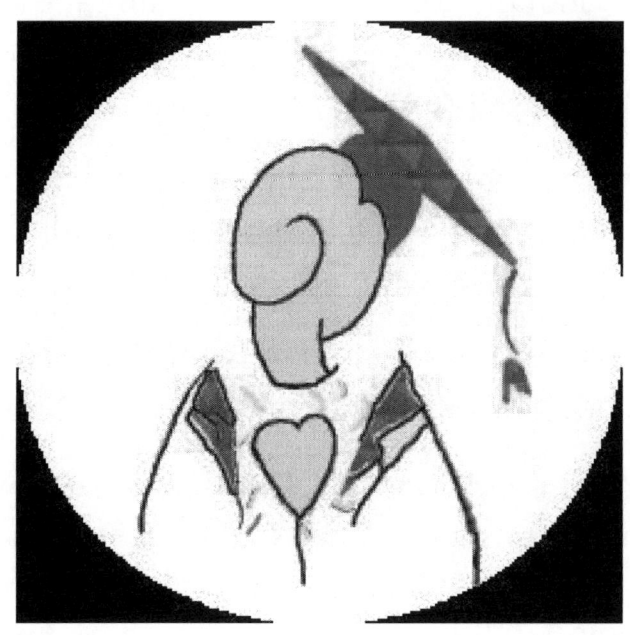

RE SELF-DISCOVERY?

Starting early on, the young individual feeling increasingly accepted, can more freely express and amplify their talents. Many 4-year-olds say astounding things. Let's welcome them. Adults, by showing delight in each contribution, especially the wayward ones, watch how children blossom. Although presently in the UK 'baseline assessments' of 4-year-olds are not mandatory (yet); the DfE adherents have an approved list of what matters (to them; for them; by them). Even though advertised as 'fun' and 'friendly', such decisive ways of quantifying the qualities and potential of our youngest citizens cause stress.

No wonder an increasing number of Reception teachers and others are calling for the removal of such assessments. Indeed, they have been lobbying hard against baseline tests.

For a complementary approach to diagnostic skills, please don't skip ATMA's offering named EARLY INKLINGS' EMPORIUM.

With all ages, in all conditions, let all matters be openly discussed and explored, even terrorism. Contentious issues can more easily become diffused when ventilated democratically, with understood differences accepted, rather than crushed by imposed edicts without consultation. Children I have found are never too young to enjoy having their contributions found to be helpful. Natural curiosity more than caution increases individual productivity.

This is not just to keep specialisations away from the mainstream but to amplify their value by a rich variety of supplementary offerings. As in a classroom, the skill is to weave their wayward contributions into the theme of the lessons in progress.

This shows us all, as with love, so also with Creation at large, all elements of existence are interrelated and therefore nobody or no thing is truly isolated or, indeed, arbitrary. In all of life's lessons the central subject is in all ways YOU! (Discuss?)

A real-life memory already published by the Independent Newspaper, might help. Forget 4-year-olds, the following recollection made an indelible impression one a 2-year-old! Let Hannah Bettany, a Christian prison outreach worker, express this in her own words:

'I remember sitting in the back of my mum's car listening to a cheesy Christian tape that went 'Born again...born again, born again.' As an example of early 'recognition', this child it seems was intuitively sensing her own life's journey. As a friend of Jesus she now feels a far less spiritually isolated adult.

How to make this personal achievement fitting to each in Self-chosen terms is the essence of all you will read here. At any age we can make more benign and bespoke choices to change our lives for the better. To help early appreciation of natural - and inspirational - modes of Self-expression, we at ATMA offer the Busy Bee Alphabet, an interactive, multimedia way of learning through movement, music, rhythm and rhyme. All of these options can fit the practical needs of the prevailing culture.

All of this and much more in later chapters..

TRUDY'S TROUBLESOME TRIBE

Like telepathy, consciousness is ageless. Parents, mostly without training, are a child's first teachers. All good lessons are reciprocal and indeed, one dad built like a butcher, admits to being 'terrified' of his 4-year-old daughter, Trudy. Told off by him for disturbing his work desk, she fixed him with a glare, one that had all the force of a frowning finger-jabbing fierce elderly judge.

Although daddy felt chastened long enough for the power play to register with father and child, adult authority got restored. Well, somewhat. Adult patience snapping, at last, Trudy was banished to the 'Naughty Step'. There, as in all subsequent rejections, she is joined by Bobby. Her younger brother kept coming to comfort Trudy, whether or not she wanted it. What will happen when Trudy is subjugated to a school still stuck in the past? Traditional schoolteachers you are warned!

Would young Trudy not sense imposed lessons as an intrusion into her private and sacred inner realms? Plato stated, 'Imposed education will never stay in the Soul'. The following imagery might be a way of expressing top-down jug-an'-mug injections of information called teaching as forms of uninvited psychic intrusion.

After all, what is Wikipedia for if not for personal and voluntary researchers of any age that proactively fizz with self-generated curiosity?

See Trudy as a hollow husk like, say, an empty low-lying bungalow. The Ofsted approach to education, aiming to prepare Trudy and her peers for the world of work, hire well-intentioned teachers to serve their own aims and objectives no matter what private objections might be held.

One twin boy Tom was comfortable with any punishment he knew he had caused. One day he gave his brother a biff and, with a grin before any tears or shouts of protest, he immediately sat himself down on the Naughty Step. The educational remit is to convert both Tom and Trudy - the lowly 'bungalows' – each into a rich and fully functional high-rise edifice.

Before full occupation is permitted, controlling adults, like property developers, 'scan' the building for any hidden treasures deemed to be unsuitable. And without consulting their potential 'purchaser'. These special gifts unique to that budding student of life are ignored or discarded - for their own good, of course. Traditional educators reckon that makes more room for every terraced 'bungalow' in their charge to be stuffed with pre-packaged fixtures and fittings, not those of the student's own choosing. (See Sandra's experience in a later chapter.) Towards that selected end product, educators train students through the narrow focus of their own over-authoritative conditioning.

Yet good lasting learning, we suggest, starts with the teacher's deep empathy for each unique student. An early blanket approach can smother the gems of embryonic individuality. Remember how one parent-teacher complained how could she decide what to teach her children until the schoolteachers had met them?

So back now to Trudy struggling to establish her true Self. Lined-up with her peers, each child in this metaphor is seen as a supposedly empty bungalow relegated into standardised over-regulated rows. Supposedly, they are made ready, willing and able uniformly, to become inhabited with ill-fitting furniture known as information.

Why? Because WE learned adults know what's best for you child, so shut up and get your head down, dear. Have we not all suffered from wallpaper patterns to which we are personally allergic; or, worse, curtains that make us cringe; or classrooms that felt like a prison cell, albeit in an open prison?

Trudy's parents did not even know that their daughter did not like her name. If Trudy had been born a peasant in one African tribe, her objection to her name might not have been a block to Self-acceptance. As a black baby, her mother would have crooned to her new little daughter all the names of their female ancestors. When the babe in arms smiled then that, for this present lifetime, was the child's chosen name. How Self-empowering is that!

So unlike a modern mum who, working at two jobs to keep the family fed and clothed,left the baby on the couch together with the mother's mobile phone. When questioned about this by her employers, she said she'd been told that to switch on white noise would help her baby to sleep. What a lost opportunity for mother-and-child bonding. In African, such a baby would be rocked to sleep in the safe and secure arms of the mother. Trouble in store...?

The African Trudy, as a newborn, as a priority would soon get introduced to all the family's livestock. Whether tethered guard dogs or goats, pet parrots or their overbearing cockerel lording itself over his harem of hens, Trudy would be accepted as a valuable part of the extended tribe within their whole family homestead.

How instructive if Trudy's Western dad had given his little daughter a personalised tour of the family's home environment. She might be introduced to the master bedroom. That might prevent a sly creep into mummy's wardrobe later, little Trudy wobbling away like a drunk in high-heels. Then in lurching on to mummy's dressing-table with many another wobble. Mum's lippy in a gash of red might get smeared across the little daughter's nose.

Well before such a possible trip back to the 'Naughty Step', Trudy and Bobby could also learn about the needs for personal privacy. In terms of space and times dedicated to personal needs, these terms could apply equally to each member of the family.

Nothing worse than burnt-out parents who puts their own needs bottom of the shopping-list, spoiling their offspring by always responding to their every demand. Parental exhaustion is no accolade. Personal space and time is best nourished by Self-chosen occupations. For a typical Indigo child this is no problem.

Imagine the bonding as dad explained to Trudy and her kindly youngest brother the purpose of daddy's private desk and its plethora of mysterious papers. Yes, it might curb her untutored curiosity, but all barked-out phrases starting with the dark word DON'T - like 'DON'T touch daddy's desk - are so life-denying. The natural Indigo like Trudy seeks explanations she can accept in order to contextualise and integrate all of her inner and outer experiences into a meaningful tapestry.

Direct experiences rather than second-hand explanations, as with too much traditional teaching, is anathema to the Indigo. If Trudy's central gift, interest and passion was, for instance, livestock husbandry, this drive would be far more useful to her, society at large and her future earning power, than all the quadratic equations and split infinitives said to be essential for the making of a successful living as the job markets shrink and robots laugh all the way to the bank.

DIRE DATA

The present system of left-brain curricula for too many obese consumers is creating an expensive lost world of the young - and not so young. Result, a demoralized tribe of 'failures' dismissed by mainstream educators. Recognise this scenario? A child, maybe you at school, afraid to ask a question in case of getting blamed for being wrong or stupid. What a way to crush young curiosity and creativity.

The walking wounded from the prevailing system of education now includes universities. Increasingly, they are limiting diversity of opinions. Due to PC (politically correct) attitudes, even in ancient universities, free speech is being threatened. (Saturday Telegraph, front page, 19 December, 2015).

In the UK as I write, 8.000 children under the age of 7 suffer depression. Recorded was a 5-year-old with psychiatric challenges was placed a ward for adults with mental health issues. 1 in 10 children between the ages of

6-16, are afflicted with 'mental' conditions. Worse it can take ten years before suitable treatment becomes available and that, too often, hundreds of miles away from the home of the said afflicted child. The Children's Minister, Edward Timpson MP, states that of up to a third of young offenders who have spent time in care, a high proportion of these end up with a mental health problem.

And lacking emotional maturity, they often express their anger through violence. For mental health, no GET WELL cards on sale.

But is this lack of emotional maturity their innate fault or more the culture that will tell 4-year-olds they are 'falling behind others'? Two or three years later they may be screaming, 'Don't want to go there.

School's horrible!'. Diminished into budding business savvy creators of wealth instead of being enlarged through storytelling, for example, is indeed to steal their childhood under the ugly guise of saying that pressure will help them to achieve. How? Not by fully exploring their true natures but by turning kids into state commodities.

According to the Association of Schools and College Leaders (ASCL) and the National Children's Bureau, out of 338 schools surveyed, 78% reported an increase in the number of pupils self-harming or feeling suicidal. And 55% reported an increase In levels of anxiety and stress, while more than 40% had suffered from cyber bullying. (Independent 5.3. 2015)

Up to the age of 12, 1 in 15 young people self-harm; some teenage girls experimenting with poisons, while 1 in 5 self-harm.. In January 1916, it was reported that in the previous three years, mental conditions requiring investigation had increased in number threefold. The alleged cause was financial cutbacks. Street gangs are an attempt to defend themselves against what look like impossible odds. Armed with knives they aim to rule their territory and remove what they find as threatening. One London family lost nine members of their family. On television, one of the survivors seemed to be surprised when she stated that a whole year had passed without one of her peers getting murdered.

After waiting four years for treatment, one victim of childhood sexual abuse started cutting herself. When tackled, she said it was to speed up referral to the authorities. Her next desperate ploy might be to get pregnant or, maybe, follow the teenage craze of posting explicit nude 'Selfies' through social media, these known as 'sexts'. Meanwhile, nearly half the number of practising teachers have been insulted on line, global multimedia outlets now nearer than the local High Street.

72% of youngsters in care have behavioural challenges. The majority of imprisoned criminals are unable to read and write. See the traditional delivery of education as a form of 'institutionalised abuse', and as with other forms of systematic abuse, the 'victims' usually blame themselves - even without 'believing' in the so-called 'necessary' cutbacks imposed by Social Services or in reincarnation and the eternal karmic law of Cause and effect!

How convenient for those with wealth aiming to stay in power over the 'plebs'; over, that is, society's victims who seem addicted to self-punishment. That is, children of all ages blaming themselves for failing in their school exams. But having been overruled almost since being toddlers and thereby disempowered, no wonder in their teen years they seek more aberrant ways to empower themselves. More on this later.

Meanwhile, those financially supported by the Social Services never in public blame their own provision and delivery of standardised lesson plans and their debilitating effect on countless young people. No wonder the Remedial services, as with the growing number of Recovery Colleges, thanks to NHS Foundation Trust, are in the ascendant. But given bad health in the many creates abundant wealth for the few, will they succeed? However in Cheshire, Jay Robinson a late developer with Asperger's Syndrome, was successfully steered into success as a songwriter. His praise for his breakthrough he expressed like this: 'The Recovery College recognises that everyone has some sort of secret talent so they encourage people to look within themselves.' Bravo, Jay!

Nonetheless, the point remains. Those who feel social 'failures' need a range of support systems. How much cheaper for the public purse if these unhappy hordes of the psychologically scarred 'school phobics' were introduced to learning systems that matched their unique gifts, insights and real reason for being on planet earth in these turbulent times of transition.

Increasingly, the walking wounded of education include teachers on burn-out. To quote from the Teacher Support Network, formally the Teachers' Benevolent Fund: 'Every twenty minutes , we receive a call from a teacher at breaking point.' In one year, the number of such adults: reached over 26,000. And now the Education Department is offering 'generous' 'golden hellos' to entice new recruits into the classroom.

In time of this being the employers' market, some might call these inducements, bribes. And no wonder, what with 10,000 qualified teachers, despite Brexit, choosing to work abroad. To prevent this leakage, beware, future classroom recruits. Your golden handshake is threatened to harden into leaden handcuffs.

Each free Soul whether or not of Indigo consciousness, has his or her own bespoke inner curricula, all according to their need to speed up their own karmic bank balance. For optimum health and balance, we might call this their inner ecology.

For those who find such statements off the wall of some asylum, we draw your attention to a survey on children's happiness. It was published in February, 2016. 8-year-olds in 16 varied countries were consulted as to how happy they were with their lifestyle. Romania came out top, whereas England came out as thirteenth in dissatisfaction. The main given reason for unhappiness was the duress and strain of their school regimes. As further evidence of malaise, 10.000 children run away from where they live. If reported as only 'absent', the police are not obliged to investigate.

ATMA does not claim to have all the 'right' answers. As a complementary approach to love in learning, see if you agree that, so far, we are asking at least some of the 'right' questions. Before you may choose to read on, a most surprising piece of current data. It was published the very day I was aiming to finish this first chapter.

NEWSFLASH! *Despite present-day worldwide skirmishes, there is a global downturn in acts of violence.* That includes those on battlefields. There are less deaths of combatants than in the 1960s, the decade in which cut flowers were stuck into the mouth of heavy gun barrels. Is that why newish world leaders in Greece, Italy and Canada have been dubbed with the Indigo label? Political leaders, like schoolteachers, as do we all, need to listen to our collective whispers of wisdom. Especially in these turbulent times in which trust in politicians is waning, and drones are deployed to obliterate 'innocent enemies'. Multitudes have been killed worldwide since scientist, inventor writer and politician Benjamin Franklin coined the phrase, 'There never was a good war or a bad peace'.

We at ATMA aim to aid these personal needs. Universal evolution calls us to serve only the very best potential in the individualized human spirit.

2· UNBELIEVABLE???

You best detective on your case

Above below this interface

ATMA's MINING ME

Your psychiatry

Shine your gemstones back into grace

Self-belief is Soul's trump card. But with so many selves to choose from, how do we select the day-to-day self that we envisioned in our own private iCloud, whilst its more substantial aspects of character we embody on planet Earth? Below as above? Throughout these pages, the lower self we depict here with a small 's'; whereas the aspirational higher Self we depict as here with a capital 'S' as in Soul.

Of course, most Buddhists do not believe in any real, independent entity for the human spirit; hence no permanent need for personal responsibility as a continuum throughout infinity. Unlike other beliefs that hold that Soul, like any other unit of energy, is indescribable yet adaptable to change. No growth without making individual choices.

Movement means we're alive. The more we move, the more blood sings in our veins and the heart opens itself to challenging the limits that had restricted many aspects of of our hidden selves. By hyperventilating, the senses tingle and feelings of excited expectation and exhilaration can be experienced.

After all, the word 'in-spire' basically means to breathe in. That is not just air, but by consciously inhaling, we can express the love we feel for our assorted best selves when feeling most happy and most alive. And then, while exhaling, we might like to focus on giving love back to life with feelings of warm-hearted gratitude. And for the lungs to operate at their optimum levels, no better exercise for the psyche and the body working together, than to seek more harmony in the act of singing heartily.

Hence the transformative Love Song to God, that some see and hear as the legendary Lost Chord. More on 'Sentient Sound and their Solutions' in a moment. So now, are you ever-ready every day to make better tomorrows than most of your yesterdays? In truth, are you ready to compose a better you?

Sound is the best tonic. SOUND, if seen as wisdom may we then see Light representing knowledge? Beauty, like our own version of truth, is in the eye of the beholder. How, but by activating the Third Eye??? Self-belief is already seeded in the human Soul??? Look now in your mirror…??? Picasso said "Believing is seeing." Ask now, if you will, 'Why have I just seen three lots of question-marks - repeated so often???' Pause while I give you the time to answer my own question and await your own good answer.

Good, Why good? Because it truly is yours! Fully integrated, it asks for ownership. So, you autonomous ones, after Brexit, feeling more composed now?

Well, since you're kind enough to be still reading this book, here goes with my own answer to this probing question. Oh, yes. Do look away now if you prefer to lose the value of your own answers and jump over the next three paragraphs. These are in **bold** *italics*. That makes it easier to skip over them with only a cursory scan.

The expression 'Third time lucky' hides a practical wisdom often overlooked by those not believing in karma and its balancing consequences. For some of us, the word 'lucky' is too shallow to explain the divine laws. These number far more than 10 and are not commandments. The number 10 can be associated with lower levels of learning. The word decimalisation, after all, originated in Roman times; decimalisation as such being associated with the phrase 'to decimate' - as in the number of deaths on battlefields.

Contrast these comments with the more spiritual number 12. Indirectly, this takes us back to the number 3. As we know, 3 goes into 12 4 times. Like the 12 signs in astrology, another way to discover one's life's spiritual blueprint is numerology. But why 'THIRD time lucky?' Time now my explanation.

In visualising some desired outcome, the Number One requirement is to see, feel, and to fill with emotion, the wished-for result. Number Two requirement is firmly to 'print' the picture in your mind. See it clearly as if already achieved and already tangibly real. But the reality of Third Time 'Lucky' comes about ideally on the third count; that is, in the envisioning the desired outcome. It is then essential in this practice of virtual reality, totally to release with feelings of love, trust and faith in the desired result. In that way, a Buddha-like non-attachment is in operation, together with a light-hearted carelessness as to all possible outcomes.

A paradox? Well yes, no earthly escape from the effects of duality. By letting go, we allow the Divine Will to operate according to its own laws. This truth you might well recognise in the streetwise saying, 'What goes round comes round'. Another similar piece of practical wisdom is, 'Let go and let God!'.

However, State systems reduce individuals down to numbers. Consider schoolchildren tested for their suitability as potential commercial units; and adults trapped like slaves to wages. In all such instances the economy is the Master Key, stupid. Says who? With this lack of Self-chosen indemnity, backed up by Self-esteem, no wonder folks want to escape mundane materialism and try drugs.

HOW DO WE ENDURE DURESS

BY FAKE TRIPS OUT OF STRESS

A DRUG-INDUCED HIGH

KISS GOOD HEALTH GOODBYE

A FACT DRUG PUSHERS BLESS?

Welcome back - three cheers!

Ready for a bit of fun? Here's a riddle. Guess to what the following quote refers. '...they're highly intelligent, capable of tenderness, playfulness, happiness and friendship.' Answer at the end of the chapter!

Now for some playfulness using the number 12. Ready? As this game proceeds, kindly drop any notion that numbers, like every second of time, are for ever eternally accurate down to the last bleep. That is true even with Greenwich Mean Time. That at first was calculated by the 24 hour clock. Yet on a digital radio, for example, the bleeps are a fraction late. As for the famous Big Ben in

London's Westminster, its tolling bell was two seconds late when seeing in the New Year on 1990.

At the mental level as with higher mathematics, in this universe of competing abilities, the uncertainty principle prevails as in many psychic engagements. Entities of the Astral plane can be very tricky! Think of items that vanish and then, unexpectedly, reappear later?

Allowing for some flexible variance between the numbers 11 to 13, spiritually speaking, most lives on earth advance in 12-year cycles. At around the ages of 12, 24, 36 etc Souls often have to face some significant change. At best, such changes allow for more personal growth. Jesus went into the Temple aged 12.

Although there were 12 years between the two Iraq wars, and it took 12 years before sanctions were lifted from Iran to prevent nuclear proliferation; plus the fact that war criminal Radovan Karadzic, leader of the Bosnian Serbs was on the run for 12 years, mathematical accuracy is not the most superior measurement of human activities. For instance, Margaret Thatcher was in power for eleven and a half years while Boone Isaacs, the African American woman in the male dominated film industry, worked for Paramount for 13 years. Whether or not you think cycles of the number 12 - like the circadian rhythm - are significant is, of course, a matter between you and the immutable Laws of Creation.

The Greek scholar Aristotle was the first known philosopher to systematize deductive logic. He said, 'The mathematical sciences, particularly exhibit order, symmetry and limitation, and these are greatest forms of the beautiful'. While the true Indigos might ignore quotes from the long dead ones preferring to coin their own truisms, we at ATMA could be grateful that he also said, 'Education is the best provision for the journey to old age'. But for today's Indigo, at what price does each place on the need for more autonomy?

Lectures versus creative diagnostic dialogues, which personally is the more enriching - for you - and why?

SALLY'S INITIATIVE

This little girl could clearly remember being on earth before. She had already announced to her startled grandmother that last time around they had been together, she, Sally, had been the gran's mother. This could shine a different light upon Aristotle's second comment quoted above. Sally was 'ageless'. Hence, the following anecdote.

'Miss, please don't shout at me. It hurts my ears and I'm trying to like you.' So said Sally when only 6-years-old. Her parents were amazed by their daughter's self-assurance and, as they saw it, her courage in challenging a teacher. They apologised to Sally's class teacher.

No need. Because of Sally's honest initiative, her teacher herself changed her attitude to Sally and to all of the individual infants in her charge. For that classroom, that benign outcome for all present was transformative. Just one example of an Indigo child inviting an authoritarian professional to humanize her teaching technique.

I was reminded of this inspiring episode when watching 'Who Let the Dogs Out?' on children's TV. The presenter, Zak George, a champion dog-trainer, congratulated the three children who had competed in training their pets to pull a weighty 'bone' over a good distance. He was magnanimous in his praise. After announcing the winner, Zak advised them all on how to continue to treat their dogs in future.

What he said was something like this. "Keep on encouraging them and keep loving!" This phrase could be placed on the staffroom door of all educational institutions.

Zak then added, "I learn as much from dogs as they do from me." This I see as another instructive motto; not just for dog-trainers, but for all adults, be they parents, teachers, preachers or politicians.

So what did I learn from Sally's initiative? That she, even at such a tender age, had enough Self-respect to express her needs in order to learn more in her main teacher's classes. I further suggest that, in her little heart's natural state of goodwill, Sally was not yet ready to lose her innate trust of all adults; not always an easy thing to sustain for the conscientious and perceptive Indigo child. Indeed, at that point in her emotional development, she did not need Zak's advice to 'keep loving' since it was already a big-hearted part of her nature, this virtue firmly rooted in Self-belief. What's more, I suggest

Sally's request was heeded because she did not imitate the teacher by shouting, but instead offered it with a quiet dignity.

My own 'indigo' ears were aurally assaulted big time recently in two large teaching hospitals. There I was being attended to by nurses; followed later by stays in a nursing home for two weeks and then in my own house for a further fortnight. As with too many teachers shouting as if their charges are all dense, many loud mouthed carers all but shouted as if their patients were all deaf; suchlike strident professionals are operating on auto-pilot.

Imposed coercion is the curse. Of course, we were all brought up by adults who mostly TOLD us what we wanted (ie, what they wanted of us as their 'victims') hardly ever ASKING us. No wonder line-managers are so central in decision making, their staff mostly having had any initiative they ever had when young, strangled out of them.

Let our over-authoritarian rulers know that such patronising autocratic behaviour will get stonewalled by the sensitive Indigo, as so by those of all ages on the Autism spectrum. (All of whom can be calmed by the healing hum of an alpaca. This stately animal is said to read auras and avoids all aspects of anger).

What, if anything, had Sally learnt from me? Her parents were atheists, yet she did not need to attend a Faith School of any religious persuasion to be smitten with a sudden worried concern.

With a frown, suddenly, she was asking us all. "Is the Dead Sea in heaven now?"

Now please, ask yourself how might you deal with this query. It needs patience, yes. In being too quickly dismissive, what levels of budding curiosity in the mysteries of Creation might get curtailed? I write this in the West, despite an increasing cynical secularism. Yet our teenagers, unlike many of the State's educational controllers, are asking to learn more about the world's rich range of religious beliefs and practises. While atheists, agnostics and humanists, rail against the assumed authority held over every holy flock, we suggest that Spirituality is still alive and kicking its bucket list. Yours too, we hope!

BYWAYS AS BABY HIGHWAYS

I enjoyed greeting children's surprising questions with delight. I'd then suggest they were interesting enough to hear the expanded views of the questioner. After that, we can open up the subject to all present, whatever their educational status. In short, a practice of inclusiveness like this, too often gets strangulated by over-prescriptive lesson-plans not allowing for unexpected contributions that can be so instructive and rewarding for all participants. Every 'byway' can be woven back into the 'highway' of the main theme being studied. In short, I believed in the value of each and all, no matter how small their offerings.

At least they show they're involved, not being cowed into unthinking compliance. At that level, I've yet to see a child from lack of school instruction truly 'suffering' - a favoured word used by 'know-all' adults. As if short of enough mainstream education they lose out like say, Sir Richard Branson!

The overuse of the word 'suffering' reminds us of the Protestant work ethic. That seems to suggest that 'If it doesn't hurt it can't be doing you any good.' Given the list given earlier of those crippled by the factory-like schools, let's ask this: 'Just whose educational good is being referred to here; those of our young adults; or more to preserve the image of the failing 'factories' what with 400, 000 schoolchildren, especially in socially deprived areas, being failed by an outmoded system which increasingly is no longer believed in by discerning and curious Self-motivated students and their exhausted teachers?

ATHEISTS ALSO WIN! As an imaginary newspaper headline, this exaggeration in bold print verges on a white lie. Don't we all share them often, as with cliches like 'We only live once' or 'Not much you can do about it'? Here's another example. How long since you saw a show on the radio? The need for accuracy can become an obsession; another aspect of the budding perfectionist, one whose conscientiousness can almost become a killer. High achievers flirt with these boundaries all the time.

Witness this world famous one. "Everyone played to an *unbelievably* high level" said the generous Andy Murray. (My italics).

Only he, Murray, was the champion wielding the tennis racquet. He had just won the prestigious Davis Cup for Britain. It was then nearly 80 years since Fred Perry had won that honour. How else to achieve such a prize other than by playing to the highest level?

Also in November 2015, the press celebrated another worthy winner for Britain. The heavyweight boxer Tyson Fury. He revealed his inner truth when he told journalists he always believed he was a champion. Years of hard work and practise, driven by Self-belief was necessary to manifest the world's non-religious adulation of such high-achievers. However, daily karma is more reliable than forecasts of British weather.

Shortly after gaining that world title, Fury was stripped of another of his earlier awards. The reason? Homophobic and misogynist comments. Interesting to note in how many ways the subject of homosexuality has been a threat to so many traditional institutions, despite its advantage of curtailing the world's population. Talk about natural birth control within, at best, the achievement of 'love all!' As if anything natural like love is not also eternally supernatural. Too freaky! Like in sacred soccer, rating footballers by how many home goals they score instead of playing with the spirit that everyone is giving of their best - and loving as well as they know how - regardless of the outcome. Or at least, that worthy aim is somewhere in their consciousness. Good to give the benefit of doubt, especially to our best teachers, the survivors.

Take the 2016 Olympic medallists in relation to their amazing sporting achievements. In my view, the biggest 'fib' told by them to media commentators was when they jubilantly gasped out the one word, "Unbelievable!"

Of course, for all competing athletes such a success was only possible because of regular punishing regimes of training. Just as surely, regular checks were made by competitors and their trainers by asking, 'Are we keeping on track with what you need to do to win?' Without Andy Murray and his advisors making regular checks on such details, how else could this tennis champion have been worthy enough to become Sportsman of the Year, 2015?

Yet for those who fail in their aims, this approach can seem as unreal as, say, what we feel after recovering from a nightmare. So belief is not a picture glimpsed in a daydream but a lightly held belief in the Big Picture; one clearly visualized in advance of all attempts at success; but done with the relaxation that comes from the spirit of trust without unnecessary stress. As to all competitors praying for the same victory, the world's fastest runner, Linford Christie, solved the apparent riddle this way. He believed that the athlete whose prayers were the most honest (and the least greedy?) was the one God answered.

However, he called God a 'He' and with no nod towards individual karma, As to Recording Angel, and the bespoke rewards given like everything else to us by the Holy Spirit, how limiting must be such a gender explicit depiction of the Deity. That was unlike the very non-

Indigo lad, rejecting Hinduism. At six, Raj was instructed on the range of Gods believed in by his teacher, 'Sir,' asked Raj, 'which is the best one for letting us off?'

Contrast that with the comfortably multi-faith city, Leicester. In May of 2016, despite phenomenal odds against them, their football team won The English Premier League a year after being rescued from relegation.

Another historic victory was announced on the same day. Mark Selby of Leicester won World Snooker Championship, this double achievement making it a feast day for that city.

Yes, both achievements will have earned handsomely. But as far as manager Claudio Ranieri and his winning team is noted, Leicester City unlike the more well-known soccer clubs, was not rich. That fact proved to be no impediment. In that well integrated, multi-ethnic city, its community and the worldwide attention such a victory gained, the realisation emerged that there were other facts at play. That is, other than finances. The club's owner is from Thailand and that Buddhist monks were in attendance, was indicating that it is consciousness, private and corporate, not cash, that best resonates with ever better blessings.

In all ways, believe in the best. Then 'the best' may agree with you!

Self-belief can also play its part in the passing of school tests. With one big difference. Punishing workloads in micro-managed state run institutions like education are mostly imposed. Whereas athletes choose to endure gruelling programs of training.

Politicians as if blackmailing them, terrify the plebs into believing only their system of stress-enduring workloads will deliver worldly success. Instead, better to prevent these many forms of ailments induced by early feelings of personal failure.

Financially, this aberration is impounded by funding the acquisition of "basic skills" to the detriment of potentially more basic needs for personal development. The result is overburdening the taxpayer with remedial strategies instead of diagnosing and "curing" the ills in systems not fitting the need to maximise individual skills.

MERIT BEFORE MONEY

The treasury pays out a fee for each academic bum on each academic seat by way of a bribe to keep the reluctant learners in thrall to a system that in their heart they would wish to challenge, if not reject. Unstated in systems of State control, is that they are based on implicit blackmail and financial bribery. Such temptation to fudge the figures such as the more money owned, the more choices can be 'bought'. Not a prescription for social mobility..

Wrong? Well, discrepancies in the marking system of examination boards gets mentioned later but for now, kindly count up in how many ways education could be improved if instead of money, it was based on the sheer love to learning. Personal passion focussed on

45

goals is more godly than the above State's boast no matter how many celebs, or teachers of Religious Studies call themselves atheists. Or indeed, those who dismiss Paul the common octopus. Supposedly, that creature predicted the results of the association football matches accurately, including the 2019 World Cup! Accept the hint, do you, that even a deep sea animal can be an oracle?

As private schools struggle to recruit enough paying parents, at least they aim to select students on their personal merits of character and not just because of their prowess on the sports field. The gift of individual talent cherished by all mostly provides more personal contentment. Let's allow more of it for all!

LOVE AS LEARNING

With an ATMA approach to love as learning, I witnessed a growth of pupil Self-confidence through the enjoyment of shared safaris into the unknown. The surprises that can come from lateral thinking is in keeping with this ancient adage: 'All students of life, incrementally, create their own reality.' Hence young learners, given a supportive environment, can come to believe in themselves as worthy enough to become author of their own Self-chosen success stories.

Although Self-belief in all ages here seems central, remember how many of the winning athletes both before and after their events, indicated a faith in some power above themselves. Andy Murray, the 'unbelievable' winner of a Gold Medal after his amazing defeat of the long-reigning tennis world champion, pointed to the sky while other winners crossed themselves or kissed the ground. Might these acts of gratitude not engage with another arcane piece of wisdom; namely, the phrase, 'As above, so below'?

So is there yet another semi-hidden and overarching truism operating here? For example, instead of saying, 'Seeing is believing', the inner truth might instead be that 'Believing is seeing.' If true, this truism in practice might be easily recognised by esoteric scientists like Rupert Sheldrake and the late Carl Sagan, author of the pioneering and seminal works on spiritual cosmology. In formulating personal identity, faith in action, is a central. This aided by the belief in continuous Self-improvement. Hence, in 2016, Andy Murray again become the well-deserved Wimbledon Champion with tears and smiles and a determination that second time to 'Enjoy it!'

A universally applicable piece of practical wisdom for all ages is this: before embarking on any individual endeavour, on any challenging dialogue with another; or on any another pioneering mission, if you wish for an 'unbelievable' outcome, first ask yourself to examine your motive. This first step the impulsive Sally did not need to take but it seemed that the main class teacher in her young life might have already been open to such guidance; just waiting for that new 'click' of consciousness. So what is this magical formula? Here it is offered as a probing question; one best posed before ambitiously embarking on some supposedly 'impossible' dream. Quietly ask yourself, "Is it true, is it necessary, is it kind?"

If you still doubt that personal belief systems precede earthly outcomes from such internal acts of visualization, then consider the responses of Medal Winners when interviewed. Often, after exclaiming, "Unbelievable!", the champion visualizers would mention that they had "dreamed" of such a success way back in childhood. Maybe around the age Sally was when, in wishing for a calmer classroom, a kinder environment, she then saw herself as being an agent of change. Every action starts with an image. Not by accident the phrase, 'Dreams come true'. (Please link these thoughts when later we present you with with details of ATMA's Early Inklings; Emporium).

Taking a rest from writing, I switched on the telly. Behold, a champion footballer was calling his team fans 'unbelievable'. And that after one of these fans had held high a wide banner throughout most of the preceding match. In tall dark print the banner sported one word only. Guessed which? Yes, it was the single word BELIEVE! - Synchronicity lives, OK! and for every Soul, whatever his or her system of belief. But for those awakening to the wonders of Creation, so-called co-incidences seem to appear more frequently; as April showers refresh springtime blooms like blessings. Maybe, gratitude is the most generous form of prayer; silent or said out loud as in thanking your loved ones - at least once a year! But why not keep the spirit of Christmas every day? And, by allowing in your future life the positive and productive POSSIBLE, repeat every day like a mantra your latest New Year Resolution!

Ground-shaking visions need a lot of empathy, energy, passion and practical support. Consider, for instance, the Eden Project. When mavericks unite, no ideal in fact is too big an ask. All horizons, with human ingenuity and perseverance, can be raised. As with scaling up the staves of divine harmonics. As also with vibrations, all the secrets are best experienced as both inner and outer sounds. Before exploring these, the answer to the riddle set earlier. I took the quote from a book by Sy Montgomery published by Simon Schuster. The title tells you the creature described. This is The Soul of the Octopus. Build Self-belief despite bleak odds

Build Self-belief despite bleak odds

Money a measure by making wads

But priceless and smart

is peace in the heart

Let Self-esteem outshine Synods*!*

3· SENTIENT SOUNDS

Who can prove dream pictures are true

Who your spiritual expert but YOU?

Souls' safaris unique

In Light and Sound speak

Embracing God's love song the HU

Spells, like mantras, are medleys of sounds that can shift consciousness and, in personal terms, its outcomes. Soul is said to travel on sound waves. As with the Golden Mean, spirituality can never get overruled or controlled by the multiple anomalies emanating from the academic mind of mankind. Even with the enlightened ones, knowledge keeps evolving. Whereas wisdom seems to be so integrated with the Laws of Creation as to be unchanging.

Traditionally, in Judaic culture, Biblical Hebrew contained no vowels. They were considered too sacred to write down. Yet In speech they were all activated in conversation; also in songs, of course, with Shakespeare as the most famous person to relish puns as if they hide some magical powers. How could the Song of Solomon in the Old Testament have lasted all these centuries had not the spells casts continued to omit all the vowels? It is vowels that 'spell' well; not when impoverished with this abbreviation: 'spll wll'!

Speaking of what the early Hebrew mystics called their 'magickal alphabet', to find G-d, they used to mediate on three words. Try them yourself. Here presented as in the above 'xmpl', they are shown without their vowels. The holy trinity of words the ancient Jews used in worship were 'Lrd', 'Tmpl' and 'Slnc'. Does this remind us of the abbreviations now commonly used in Tweets and Texts?

But in case you are still puzzled over the third word, it is perhaps not one beloved of musical directors trying to train a choir. Unless perhaps, the work presented before them is by John Cage. Hint accepted? The third word, as hopefully you will have guessed is, of course, 'silence'. In sound as in songs, it is vowels - considered the yin (female) to complement the more aggressive yang (male) sounds - that add a liquid loveliness to all languages.

If you don't believe this, try singing the Three Blind Mice without their vowels. Indeed, it is in using maximum breath control and in singing at the top of our voices, that the human voice can resonate with some out-of-this-world ineffable bountiful brilliance. So yes, the five vowels give poetry to words just as the colours blue, black, red, yellow and green give vibrancy to the five rings representing the worldwide Olympics.

What follows now is a way of musically scoring the five vowels. In the following exercise, every singer can find their voice and can, thereby, become 'en-chant-Ing'. However, since our characters and life experiences are so varied, and genetically and temperamentally we are all so different, certain of the five vowels will uplift our spirits more than others. And this will change with our moods. Naturally, the more we are in charge of our mood swings the more likely we are to be effective and successful in most of our endeavours.

Without Self-discipline Opera singers, for instance, would turn into emotional mush in death-bed arias; just as actors playing the part of murderers could turn into killers on stage if they were not in control of their emotions. It is through such Self-controlled artistry that we in the audience get moved. Sounds delivered in the minor key may ventilate any of our hidden feelings of self-pity. Whereas sounds expressed in the major key can open the heart and arms to the eternal joys of optimism; the very essence of evolution. What newborn springtime lamb does not leap in sheer celebration of its life? And for group cohesion, nothing better than choral singing. All the more disgraceful the cutbacks on music lessons in schools. The downgrading of music, dance and drama is what suits dictators.

Back to where we started: movements mean we're alive, especially perhaps, when moved by certain movements in a symphony composed by the sublime Beethoven. His famous Symphony Number Nine he first called 'Ode to Freedom'. Despite his romantic idealism and as a matter of political expediency, it got changed.

Too much personal freedom was usually curtailed by Kaisers and other rulers; as so today, in and out of school classrooms, even in so-called 'Free Schools'. But In Beethoven's time, the Emperor Napoleon whom at first the composer admired, was again on the move. This time, it was to subjugate the citizens of Portugal and Spain before waging war against Austria for the fourth time. No doubt, his troops 'moved' in marching order to the beat of martial music.

Despite Beethoven writing, "What a destructive disorderly life I see and hear around me: nothing but drums, cannons, and human misery in every form", the Choral Symphony was re-named 'Ode to Joy'. By then, the often exasperated composer was too deaf to hear it played or, for that matter mercifully, the drums and guns of yet more war.

But given the human being's vast range of free choices, which movements, physical, mental, religious, and political best suit our current needs? Like all other preferences, each choice helps us to define our outer identity.

This, though, is formulated within us; often in secret and often in silence. I'm sure Beethoven's inner ear was receiving melodies from heaven long after losing his hearing.

So now, inwardly and/or outwardly, please try this experiment. Out of the selected vowels that follow shortly, which sound works for - and with you - more than the others by moving you into, say, joy, sadness or feelings of inner freedom?

A friendly warning: in English, as with the word 'Amen', the letter 'a' can be pronounced to rhyme with the words 'hay' and 'neigh' and - so confusing for foreigners - also with the way the words 'half' and 'daft' are pronounced. Hence, the 'a' can rhyme with your 'ma' and 'pa' as well as with your 'mate' and 'mater'.

Why not try all these alternatives as also with the fifth vowel, the 'U'. Likewise, this vowel can be pronounced as in our word 'hUman' or, alternatively, as in the word 'hUg'.

Life is full of choices and if we don't make them, then they are more likely to be made for us by some 'Napoleon'. But our own inner music of wisdom's magic remains untouchable, beyond the reach of all would-be tyrants. Now if you will, sing and or chant each vowel in turn as outlined below:

'A' as in 'ma' and/or its alternative pronunciation, 'Hay'.

'E' as in 'healing'.

'I' as in the friendly greeting 'Hi'.

'O' as in 'holy' and 'golden'.

'U' as in 'human' and/or as in the word "hum".

My invitation to you can be extended by experimentally taking each vowel in turn. Intone them up and down the musical scale. (If you're an overweight opera singer, you might even sound better on your bathroom scales!)

If and when you wish to incorporate bodily movements as with ATMA's Busy Bee Alphabet, while exhaling the breath on your chosen musical notes, why not create a range of expressive movements?

These might be borrowed from gymnastics; or you might feel sufficiently moved to invent gestures to greet the sun, followed by sending salutations to the four directions of the compass, North, South, East and West. Perhaps add to those gestures ways of showing thanks for your five senses; hearing, sight, touch, taste and smell.

To crown all these exercises, maybe the best idea yet is this: relishing in turn the sound of each vowel in your whole name. Articulate it with a smile while admiring yourself in your bedroom's looking-glass. And if obstinate shadows still darken your tones, try using the Law of Manifestation.

That is, invite your Higher Self to bless you with some unconditional glittering showers of golden magic. Ironically, to let this marvel to manifest, it is best to drop all anxiety and to stop looking for what you want. It might not be what you need!

Blessings, like golden notes, are earned through surrender; not therefore by passive folks, but by the proactive ones working in loving harmony with the impersonal laws of the universe.

WIDE OPEN SCHOOL

Slovakia is where I was asked to run a teacher training program by the Head of the above named school. Kill the child in the adult and you often slaughter the capacity for wonder and FUN - again short for FUNdamental.

 What follows now is how I introduced little learners to the magic of the five vowels:-.

As the music plays, see yourself moving like a butterfly, or drawing one in beautiful colours.

ON OVERHEAD PROJECTOR SHOW:

26 LETTERS OF THE ENGLISH ALPHABET! EACH LETTER IS MAGICALLY IMPRINTED ON A BUTTERFLY'S WINGS.

MIGHT IT SEEM THAT, WORLDWIDE, AS A RESULT OF THESE MARKINGS ON SO MANY FLYING INSECTS FROM A RANGE OF DIFFERENT COUNTRIES, THAT THERE WAS THE INTENTION TO SIGNAL ENGLISH AS A GLOBAL LANGUAGE?

FAVOURISM MASKING PREJEDICE? OH DEAR, HOW POLITICALLY SUSPECT – AND AFTER BREXIT, TOO!

THAT SAID, FOR EASY READING BY ALL OF THE WORLD'S CITIZENS, IN A VARIETY OF VIVID COLOURS, THEIR WINGS ARE DISPLAYED SPREAD WIDE SO GENEROUSLY THAT EACH ONE COULD FEATURE ON PAGE 3 OF 'THE INSECT GAZETTE'!

Ready for the next amazing gift from Mother Nature?

Astonishingly, this colourful display also shows on butterfly wings the numbers 1 TO 9. Awe is not strong enough to express our astonishment and gratitude.

These wonders in full are displayed in full on the next page.

ENJOY!"

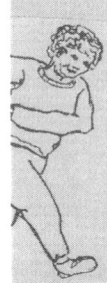

FIG. I

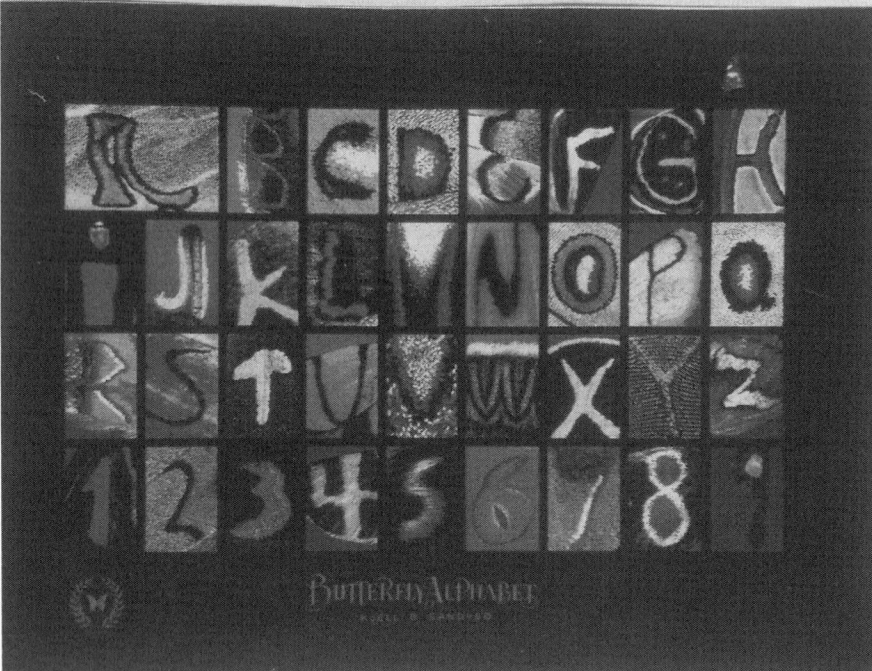

Nature's Alphabet

*Since ancient times, scribes and calligraphers have lovingly depicted the alphabet
in illuminated manuscripts, printed books and chiselled on stone, but never before have
the letters and numerals been presented as written by nature's own hand.*

Meanwhile, back in Slovakia:

Here there are lots of coloured pens. When you are ready, select 3 colours, and then collect a white card. Then, using your chair as a table, draw a coloured butterfly while I tell you a story about the five vowels, A,E,I O and U.

'I am the TALLEST!' said I. 'So I should rule in this school. I should,' said I, loudly. 'Oh no, oh no,' said O. 'I'm the best Vowel - bravO!' 'Eh, eh, eh,'said A. 'There's going to be a fight. Good!' 'I'm easy,' said E. 'You lot,' said U. 'I'm the smartest, you see. I don't like fights. So, see you! I'm off…' And U ran off down the road…

At the next crossroads, U was met by a beautiful Butterfly. 'Life's too short to cry, little one. Let's do a U-turn'. With that, the Butterfly led U back to the other 4 vowels who were still fighting amongst themselves as to which one was the best vowel. Seeing the beautiful Butterfly, they all fell silent. 'This is my friend,' said U. 'This beautiful Butterfly will tell us all how to become more open and happy'. And he did. What secrets do you suppose this Butterfly shared with them all…?

FREE FAITH SCHOOLS

In consciousness, personal faith is central. Yet we do not consciously need to 'believe' in oxygen - or a divine Creator - to stay breathing. Those who aim to 'convert' us, notice how repetitious is their learned-by-rote phrasing and how loud their voice. Inner uncertainty sounded ever thus. The fear of isolation means that often we seek companionship, fruitful or unsuitable, wherever it can be found. And the condition for bonding? A shared belief system, one often called a religion.

What might a 'Free Faith School' founded by ATMA Enterprises present as its prospectus?   Well, please read on.

Mainstream educational provision may well protect its own constraints, like vested interests. Because of successful public relations, the idea is that the uneducated masses feel they have no successful future prospects unless jumping through the state's academic hoops, even when students take up apprenticeships or vocational courses. The fear of failure is what would keep the majority of parents and their offspring, stakeholders in this sterile and mostly secular materialistic mainstream system of servitude. The price? Staying shackled by purse-strings mostly held by politicians in collusion with the multinational money manipulators. Understandable though are these restraints, this way to worldly success is seen as mandatory by the majority of well-meaning adults afraid of anyone in the family becoming penniless. All this rush, stress and distress is endured as if no alternatives are available. So what is offered throughout these pages is a more complementary approach to the State's provision, aided by sessions of direct experiences, all crafted by and with students, each to further discover yet more depths in his or her own true nature, interests, gifts and skills; these the lodestone of their personal power. Nothing new under the sun, for sure. But a harsh system need not lead to harsh interactions between all ages of learners. Witness much good practise in state nursery schools. Is it ever too early to allow all choices, including thoughts, attitudes and actions, to have consequences that are instructive? Ideally, this vast and unique toolkit of human potential is driven by Self-awareness in action at its wisest best. All experiences can be aiming for more meaningful Self-advancement in order to add all of our creative gifts to the cornucopia of human productivity. To achieve that, know you can reach every goal your good heart's desire can target.

Personal responsibility comes from the way we each respond to our inner and outer environment. If learners become ill-at-ease with their outer life, then their inner sense of Self can become diminished and youngsters' lives become bleak, empty and meaningless. They can then feel as blank as an out-of-date bank note. Yet participation in more Self-selected studies, piecemeal, demonstrate personal aspirations and aptitudes and, as in the training of child athletes, artists and scientists, establishing social prestige and innovate autonomy. That is, rather that than apathy. So far, no curriculum known to me in the UK, suits the Indigo consciousness. Read on if you will, and with our loving ATMA Team, unpack the treasures awaiting the attention that turns participants into better, more useful and beautiful human beings. And as for any of you still uncertain as to what we mean by the term Indigo, GOOD. Surely that means you're already keen to keep on reading!

INCENTIVES AND PENALTIES

To facilitate ATMA's elevated aims requires that all students of life-long learning are encouraged to enjoy their innate gifts, interests and skills through experiences in stress-free and safe settings that increase Self-awareness through a variety of options. By being invited to prioritise their choices early on, aspiring learners are continuing to define their unique nature. For balance, give periods of ethical reflection for each 'playmate' of whatever age. This respite allows the next wave of insights to inspire the creative processes to function faster and more fruitfully in ways that have been called 'educational fun'.

Taking charge of their total energetic 'tool-kit' also hones Self-managed disciplines; and when fired by personal enthusiasm, expected achievements become their own bespoke rewards. Given so many ways to ENJOY learning, when older, Self-confidence, based on their core of Self-certainty already established, can help them deal with matters less personally comfortable as life's unpredictable and challenging circumstances arrive to test and to extend them.

Within any range of individual characters, we all have special needs because each is indeed special. And an indelible Indigo knows it! Ideally, without an overweening ego. Initiative and innovation in the spirit of the inventor already inborn, these struggling entrepreneurs who may not yet be able to pay themselves a salary, nonetheless persevere. Such proactive Souls, such incorrigible hotheads are likely to achieve more than the conditioned average person. Given this Self-confidence, even without support, can drive ever more successful outcomes. On their own terms.

But is this encouraged? No. Take this government policy in the pipeline. Business accounts have soon to be submitted every three months to the Income Tax instead of once a year. The exchequer already receives thousands of pounds in penalties levied on those who miss the current January deadline. Imagine how much more they are surely expecting with glee to rake in if this new policy gets into law?

Nearing his old age, the ever-questing Albert Einstein, still staying creatively curious about all of existence, said, "Knowledge can take you from A to B, but imagination can take you round the whole globe'. The individual quester, having conquered many tasks and discarded many earlier theories, when confronted with say, an animal or an abstraction; a book or a Bunsen burner; a classroom or cloned robots; let alone choosing between a pen and a PC, today's Indigo 'Einsteins' know that, in many tasks, the Self-managed computer will beat the human brain.

Unless confronted with a genius who might indeed be Autistic. This vast spectrum includes folks with Asperger's syndrome. These conditions increasing in number as consciousness continues to rise, with ever younger geeks programming our domestic and industrialised automated maids'.

Self-evolving computers are postulated by no less an eminent thinker than professor Stephen Hawking. Imagine a herd of future semi-sentient, semi-autistic robots not believing in their creator, mankind. Worse, might a roving herd of atheist robots become serial killers, imitating the most destructive of their human murderers? For those thinking out of the box, political correctness is not productive.

Another profound inner explorer, Paul Dirac, the pioneer of quantum theory, was said to have distinctly passed every criterion of autistic bravura. Am I alone in sensing a quantum connectivity between Quantum Consciousness and, subliminally, those on the Autistic/Indigo spectrum? A materialistic, mechanistic uncreative curriculum is anathema to all of them.

Those with any form of spectrum 'disorders', like dyspraxia or sensory processing, being overwhelmed can become violent. That often leads to exclusion from school, the number of rejected early 'failures' growing since 2006. What if it is these acutely sensitive Souls in pain were instinctively rejecting the system as to them being profoundly unsuitable? Nurtured in a less didactic and prescriptive regime many thrive. With bespoke individualised care - culled by universal state cutbacks - many school 'rejects' have become useful to society at large, their niche skill-set fully in operation.

If only our benighted rulers would honestly admit that the old world of many choices in the job market is shrinking. The result being there will be more 'enforced' free times from paid employment. Hence, the Finnish government's policy of giving each member of its society a standard monthly allowance called Citizen's Income. As in my New Age novel faction, ALICE IN WELFARELAND, this state intervention is designed to replace dependency on the Welfare State with more personal responsibility; this all but enforced by changing circumstances. The Finnish term for this is Play Remit. You will have noticed how often we are using the word play instead of work. Hence, let's be happy to help others see the need to have creative hobbies and to nurture such interests from early on as part of that person's private curriculum.

But ATMA'S Sue Bayley cautioned us with these wise words: "Often your first experiences of learning and play can have bitter sweet memories. Conditioning from parents, teachers and peers can terminate the desire to learn, and reduce Self-esteem, and decisions to trust self and others. In essence, my muddles and struggles in life, have forced me to create strategies, for learning who I am, what my life purpose is; how to cope in a neuro-typical world, when I am in the Autistic spectrum, and how to be cognisant in Somatic, Emotional, Cognitive and Spiritual intelligences. Best to free up your inner child, by un-learning old habits, through play, and re-activate creativity, passion and joy".

Unstructured play can be treated as another nourishing life-long ingredient to feed the spirit. Ideally, introduced as a pre-emptive strategy. This was not the case for a doctor's grandson who we'll call Henry. This 7-year-old was still unable to read. Not a concern if Henry was in Finland. But in England, with its exaggerated dirge, the politicians' alarmist theme song of 'Don't let our children's education suffer,' the difference is not just stark but damaging to many children who could have gained more learning by being home educated; another area of self-development threatened as our rulers excuse their restrictive policies by exaggerating the fears of terrorism.

But back to Henry. By way of an expensive and remedial reaction to his supposed illiteracy, he was diagnosed as in need of a Play Therapist. Given the lad was allowed to lead the sessions, all according to his latest interests, within three weeks Henry was reading without difficulties. Who says a playful approach is unimportant? Autonomy, deja vu and love of learning with ever-expanding Self-expression allowed to flourish, the results of such nurture are at best transformative.

Let's finish with a quote from Einstein in relationship to a playful approach to learning. He said, 'Play seems to be the essential feature in productive thoughts - before there is any connection with logical construction.'

Now for a repeat of our ATMA aphorism; namely: Love links; mind thinks; fear shrinks - Soul knows!

The Finnish attitude to schooling, like the economic policy outlined above, is likewise innovative. Indeed, their ministers might like to read my updated version of Alice as she tests the tetchy impatience of the academic owl perched at the top of his tree. The bough on which he perches is bent low with too much heavy learning.

Challenged from below by my Alice, this runaway Convent girl insists, 'Mr Owl dear, kindly praise me. I'm being provocative again.' In memory of Martin Luther at Wittenberg, she is on the way to Humpty Dumpty, boss of E.M.B.E.R.S, the 'bloated bantam's egg' who presides as Education's Mortar-Board Eggzamination Remarking System.

To this smug lecher Alice presents a tract for the reformation of schooling. It is not a million miles from the current Finnish model.

AUTHENTICATING ANECDOTES

By supplying a whole alphabet of kindly but contrasting stimuli, each student's record of what subject is imposed and for how long interest is sustained, is so Self-revealing that their obvious need for personally compatible studies can become amply demonstrated. Not all fruit trees will bloom in the same soil.

To those involved, personal anecdotes are unique evidence, each one bespoke to that person's response to experiences. And it can start in the kid's high-chair. Consider this parent to a toddler who would not eat up his vegetables, saying. "This is what I want you to do." (Parent mimes eating cabbage.)

Consider the toddler replying. "This is what I want you to do." Folds arms in defiance. The need for autonomy is greatest in the most developed Souls. Hence, to those with an Indigo consciousness, the word 'irrational' as in discourse, is no more an insult than is the belief of unseen formative yet invisible energies like imagination.

As with the experiences of mystics, no scientist will persuade them that their voices and visions are not real - on one level or another. Imagination cannot be measured in a test tube.

As love has many levels, so also has a rich inner life of the private heart and Soul, whether or not dismissed as mere imagination.

Even in China, never mind employers in Microsoft, 'fact slaves' are not being selected. More in favour now are employees with a capacity of fantastic thinking as in bedtime creative storytelling.

Good news for those accused of their religion being based on fiction. Maybe tales of personal miracles and medical marvels will soon not get so easily dismissed as insignificant anomalies.

What follows now is just one of many anecdotes gleaned from the varied fields of learning in which I have shared in four Comprehensives in the UK as well as in numbers of institutions in ten countries abroad.

6-year-old Stephen, in rejecting traditional schooling, was taken to smaller classes in which the working ethos was one of 'Shining Eyes and Busy Minds'. There, creative approaches to personalised philosophy were on offer; together with other activities like Clowning Skills, Brain Gym and interactive Storytelling. Very soon Stephen told his committed teachers and parents that such Saturday morning classes were 'Magic medicine!'

For a healthy society with a Self-fulfilling future for each and all, worldwide, as an ideal the 'happiest days of your life' have flown out of classroom windows, together with the daydreams of disenfranchised students.

Might not the dark roots of depression start to deepen as youngsters meet controlling adults who would denigrate most of the kid's most precious insights and experiences?

Except in exceptional cases, demoralisation is bound to follow. Education should be making each student feel exceptional. Indeed, we would be delighted to explore these issues further with you in order to bring back a sense of idealism and vocation; not just in teachers but in learners of all ages.

For reference, The Routledge International Handbook of Philosophies and Theories of Early Childhood Education and Care; (Edited by Professor Tricia David, Kathy Goouch and Sacha Powell). Educators from all round the world are featured; including myself on sharing philosophy with +4-year-olds which I enjoyed for ten years in London.

APPREHENSIONS

Given you can recall your earliest impressions, how significant for you are your earliest memories, in or out of your latest womb? Where did they come from and why? Is it possible these lingering impressions were, in some weird way, predictive? In addressing such questions, do you not long for more sacred answers to life's multiple mysteries; those that keep we questers not cowed too long with humiliating modesty. Better by far is to fire the ambition to understand whether or not, for instance, there is a gene for curiosity? Or is that also yet another false lead...?

The psychologist Oliver James found that most explanations of human characteristics cannot be found in the gene pool; missing ingredients unidentified. While the scientific mind seeks replication of results, the exceptional, like the anomaly, will always pose a threat to that rational requirement. If there is no indisputable explanation for human outcomes at the cellular level, what about at the supernatural level? Are we mystified by the phase 'hidden in-heritability'?

Or even by the 'Missing Link' or the 'Lost Chord.' Yet inexorable laws of Cause and its consequential repercussions seem to prevail. Many believe these are k3pt above, that our spiritual records get presenting to us later, like gas bill. Yet some will claim that if we ask the Universe, we each can learn how our Highest Self can reveal these to us through the Recording Angel. Akasha, a Sanskrit word accepted by Western teachers and informing the channelled book of 1908, *The Aquarian Gospel of Jesus the Christ*, a text well worth researching.

Years back I met a dull man sitting in an upright chair. Having lost several jobs he was bemoaning how fickle was his private fortune. Probably adults had not suited his inner needs. Result, a necessary nervous breakdown. There seemed to be no way out of his pall of misery and despair. But wait...light can always loom out of the gloom.

Beside his chair I spotted a pile of books. They were all on aspects of personal transformation. Pointing at them, 'Is not this your real life's work, Noel?' I asked. 'If so, why not recall your first childhood dreams of what you wished to become...?'

Multiple Olympic medallist Max Whitlock with hands and arms that send him spinning around in a series of giddy oscillations around his pommel horse in his youth made an imprint of his hands. Alongside them he wrote a predication. He knew they belonged to a future Olympian champion. Another case. As a youngster, to her sister, Teresa May announced that one day she would be the prime minister! In the next chapter, please explore with us.

4 EARLY LEARNERS KNOW LOTS!

May life be blessed as love allows

No old Soul to falsehood bows

An INDIGO child

Will not be beguiled

Staying true to pre-birth vows

If I asked you how you learnt your alphabet, I bet you can't remember. Right? Is that because learning it was more a boring chore than a jolly chortle?

Now another question. For you, educationally, what qualities might the letters ABC stand for?

Oh sorry. If you are an 'Indigo', you might have expelled a sigh of pity for the poor adult, parent, teacher or even author who asked you to answer such an 'obvious' question. The Indigo, be it an adult or a child, hearing that certain tone of voice might feel patronised.

Recognise that feeling? Like me, have you not met middle-aged toddlers who stare at you as if you're unhinged?

Take Jack's mother. One day her son blurted, "I've lived in all ages, left eyes everywhere and can see everything." Pause as Jack staring at the fridge door not his mum, added, "Want an ice-cream now!" Not a question, notice. More an imperative. After all, isn't it obvious the child CAN have an ice-cream? Jack had seen them get placed in the fridge after a boring traipse round the local supermarket.

So no need to obey silly rituals and parrot a 'please' after the demand. Obvious! What's more, his family's pets never say 'please' either, do they? Or say 'thank you' after scoffing more than their share. One 4-year-old girl accused of being possessed by an evil spirit, her local priest insisted on an exorcism. In her house to administer such, the youngster, not witnessed by parents, gave the robed celebrant a deeply penetrating gaze as she said, 'You don't have to go on your knees and wear a frock to talk to God...'" Never to seen again by that family, the priest fled from the house.

OLD SOULS

Ageless Indigos are born 'Knowers', no matter how irritating that is to others. Or that is the impression they can project. Jack, sending his mum into a spin of anxiety she'd given birth to a freak who'd end up as one of life's failures, Jack got his ice-cream. And his age at that time? 4-years-old. But it's this sense of unshakable 'knowing' that often sets Indigos apart, even from their families.

How do I know this?

Only nine years old I was, walking through a field of flax. I was with a female companion, one a good twenty years older than me. As we walked along side by side in a companionable silence, suddenly she looked down on me and announced, "You're an Old Soul." Without hesitation I replied, "I KNOW!".

A few steps further on and, puzzled, I came to a halt. Not having understood what I had just blurted, I asked the lady to explain. She could not. Instead, she explained that somehow she just 'knew' it to be so. That made two of us with Indigo-like symptoms. But now as an adult educationalist I have come to realise something I see as significant. After that moment of recognition, me ambling along unthinkingly in the countryside, my conditioned schoolboy's brain kicked in. How had I dared to assert myself like that? Arrogant or what? After all, till that moment I had never heard the phrase 'Old Soul', let alone understood it.

I repeat; your answers to any of life's many riddles is more valid than mine, once you claim responsible ownership of such. Nonetheless, I still will invite you to explore with me other interpretations. Now though, let me proffer another set of seemingly imponderable, yet interconnected, conundrums. Can an iceberg 'understand' vapour? Again, can either an iceberg or vapour 'understand' running water? See what I'm NOT saying here, only implying...?

Why, does not water contain a trinity of transformative properties? Water can stay frozen; flow away and rise to its own level like human love even without us being baptised. Alternatively, water can evaporate. These three states, all according to its environment, can manifest. Contrast that with human cogitation. As, for example, in debating the elusive balance between the competing influences of nature and nurture. What percentages of each might apply to us as 'water-carriers'? Are we not versatile enough to produce an infinite number of variables? Water's three states of being are more curtailed by only its physical environment. But as Soul, are we contained, let alone constrained by our physicality? Certainly not. Otherwise for us humans, no clear epiphanies, transformations or miracles are ever possible.

Yet within our humanity an invisible wheel is involved. Think of condensation. Thanks to the water-wheel, vapour can reappear on earth as liquid drops shimmering as dew on the morning lawn. Maybe as a symbol of reincarnation. If this is indeed the true situation for Soul, the implications are cosmic. How, but by using Earth as our main classroom, life itself is offering us all lessons that we can turn into blessings.

What relief to 'know' through direct personal experiences. How refreshing on the break of daylight to run barefoot through newly dappled grass as our naked toes scatter delicate dewdrops like liquid sparks? Suddenly, remarkably, incontrovertibly, every single thing is exactly as it should be, all according to the laws of Creation!

As guidance would have it, in a car on ATMA business with one of our team, David Renner, we talked about fresh water, that invaluable mainstay of life. We asked, How long before such daily commodities like bread and water gets sold on the black market? David mentioned that in the United States where droughts are common as in California, they place black plastic balls on the surface of their reservoirs. With no rainfall forecasted, that reduces the risk of condensation. In me, that image morphed into black spots as on roads where traffic crashes are most frequent and police photographs (unpublished), often reveal phantom faces at the scene of fatal 'accidents'.

In human terms, I then thought about my spiritual blind spots. The ones that might make condensation (reincarnation) on my next round on the water-wheel of life less likely. You, too? Then let's further explore more parallels between the three states of water, these in relationship to the human condition.

CHOSEN PARENTS?

Ready to ask your Highest Self some more Soul-searching questions? Answers to your own Self-selected questions produce Self-defining answers. From that truism, one might say that 160 selective grammar schools are, after all, on the right track despite accusations they do not boost social mobility. With one big proviso. What if students of all ages are encouraged to see the advantages of consciously defining themselves by each learning to select her or his own schools, subjects and teachers? This complementary (spelt both ways!) approach, we at ATMA Enterprises, like yourself hopefully, truly relish.

Responses invite personal responsibility. Who better to answer all of life's central questions - questions like What is the main purpose of MY life? - than the questioner? Indeed, our team at ATMA is conducting research along these very lines; the like of which are described more fully in references to MINING ME. Meanwhile, ready to probe more deeply if your own life is fit for purpose?

How many incidents can you recall from early childhood? Due of pain, are they 'frozen' in time? Alternatively, if you are now living 'in the flow', have those memories, painful or not, 'evaporated'? Importantly, if not, why not? Or do they still linger like lumbago? If so, is it because such memories signify some neglected aspects of your birth plan causing ever more stress?

You see, we believe that before we're born, under guidance, we agree to our next body, our next gender, family unit, its culture and country. All chosen, no matter how tough life on Earth is to be, to maximise our spiritual learning potential. That is to eschew the cliches, 'You only have one life'; 'You don't choose your parents'; and 'I didn't ask to be born!'. For the Indigo consciousness, the other cliche, 'No problem', means exactly what the words say. Karmic debts no longer prove a burden when we happily agree to pay every bill. And thank the post-person!

Given that whatever we were strong enough to cause in our past, we must therefore be strong enough to cure in the present. Such is the equation of Cause and effect getting ironed out by our own volunteered actions, as each becomes willing to balance the books. And the sooner the better.

Can we see this liberating possibility as predestined? With our pre-birth permission? If so, let's see if there was a list of these guidelines on our self-chosen path as signposts and crossroads, all arranged on our behalf before again we got reborn.

Established as such, that scenario can be accepted as our current contract with Spirit. Happy consequences should be the result. Like collectors of so-called 'coincidences'. I trust you have already been experiencing a number of magical moments of déjà vu? I thought so, for such flashes of recognition happen in old Souls of all ages; think of little Jack stating he'd lived in all ages.

INTIMATIONS

All choices have consequences, of course. And spiritual amnesia is widespread. So what about the veil that allows us to 'forget' most of our past choices? Yet is it not when certain situations become 'unbearable' that we can make breakthroughs in terms of Self-acceptance? It seems that the godly love that gifted us with free will remains valid at all levels for Soul's growth. Until, that is, spiritually we ripen enough to reclaim our fullest fruitfulness and the freedom that comes from unconditional acceptance.

Then, each time back in earth's classrooms, at every crossroad, 'recognised' or not, we still have free will. Yes, at every crossroads we can choose to go forwards, backwards, left or right; downwards or upwards. For the Indigo consciousness, standing stuck in our own muck is not an option! Hence our exploring further here the idea of 'Early Inklings'.

Intimations of future events as with Prophets and Seers are well-known, no matter to the cynical seeker they might seem merely anecdotal.

In this age of secular scientists and the other worldly pundits influencing public opinion, I am saddened that personal anecdotes, like case histories that do not fit the remit of any presiding researcher, get dismissed as invalid.

Like an unintended insult, I experienced this with one Northern university. The researcher was exploring attitudes to life, death and much in between. In the final paper, my references to reincarnation were not included. Redacted. Rejected as irrelevant, Just like reports of children discoursing with invisible friends.

How tempting for the child to mislay his or her sense of reality and its multiple layers of experience as others dismiss such happenings as 'mere imagination'. But imagination has preceded everything that exists, including our temporary clouds of unknowing.

EARLY LEARNERS KNOW LOTS

One eleven-year-old I taught asked, "How many dimensions has imagination?" "Stephan, what a fantastic question,' I said. 'You're obviously well tuned-in'. 'Yeah,' nodded Stephan, 'not even the girls call me stupid!'

Stupid? Like KISS - Keep it Simple, STUPID? Being dyslexic like one in ten people, Stephen was sick of being accused of being 'stupid'. Yet he was already able to frame cosmic questions like a budding physicist. A fortnight later, to my horror, I learnt that Stephen had been 'statemented'. That is, by left-brain teachers he was rated as 'educationally subnormal'. Hence the boy was relegated to the remedial 'thickies'; albeit with one-to-one counselling.

Dejected, there he languished like a factory reject of no commercial use. There, like the sensitive and insightful Soul that he was, Stephen despaired. That had me wondering how such kindly teachers can outlaw their non-linear learners with such a lack of insight. It made me think that the richer the consciousness, the slower its fullest flowering. Most awakened folks I know who show more intuitive cosmic awareness than worldly knowledge were late developers like Stephen.

They need person-to-person nurturing. This would seem a drain on the public purse. Which is why certain primary schools have forty little ones in one class. But, what about the expense to society as those not individually helped to mature when young, as adults, are thrown on the refuse heap of humanity unable to support themselves. Remedial services are more much expensive. But such jobs hype the employment figures.

By rote, it's supposedly easier for 'parrots' to learn the alphabet and times tables, than it is to apply their rich range of applications. So educationally, we might see the truest and longest lasting curriculum is that of our own personal consciousness. The Indigo student, rather than regurgitate lists of facts that do not 'connect' with the needs of his or her inner development, will refuse to stay stuck to the assembly-line of compliant learners. Given that Indigos have already spent centuries mindlessly repeating their ABC and 123, no wonder 'boring' today becomes the children's favourite classroom swearword.

Subliminally, what we each yearn for, is to express our present gifts; to peruse them with passion; to develop our interests in more detail; to live inside out ever more fully, and all this to be achieved in order to find out all the reasons we are back on earth again. Those with ATMA Enterprises are happy to explore each and every ingredient of our own Master Learning Menu. Such pro-active levels of awareness are not known in most mechanistic school systems with a materialist agenda.

While working in state schools without a university degree, I came to see everyone, all students, parents and teachers including me, as needy children. Many were unhappy. Maybe because not expressing their own special core gifts. This attention and care of the true Self can save sanity from collapse and prevent stress from firing diseases. Never too early to bring full flowering our personal childhood gifts and offer them to the world like a bouquet. (See my dvd, Early Learners Know Lots. It is on the ATMA website.)

Is it too speculative to suggest that the deeper the nosedives into a materialistic culture the higher the desperate incidents of mental despair?

The ageless Indigo is often the opaque one on the fringe of the family and society at large. When slow to develop, such a person can get diagnosed as somewhere on the autistic spectrum. Yet eventually, if not sooner, the true Indigo shows an unshakable belief in themselves as supernatural heirs to their own well-deserved Kingdom. That might be cosmic in scale or, as is often the case, a narrow focus is earnestly concentrated as if a sunbeam though a MAGNIFYING-glass, on one specialised subject area. It is almost as if that Soul had already experienced most that life can offer already but, significantly, any past blind spot left unattended to now needs concentrated attention.

Alternatively, that Soul may have chosen a path of service for the betterment of mankind. In every case, the 'oddballs' like orphans amongst us need to be cherished. As for the Indigo foundling, that Soul might have chosen the chance to experience Self-parenting, a possibility that we at ATMA would love to explore further with you.

LEARNING BY HEART?

Have you yet remembered how, where, when and with whom you learnt your ABC? Me, neither. Could it be because it was not enjoyable? We at ATMA Enterprises re-coin certain traditional terms to signal a complementary approach to whole person love as learning. Education, for example, becomes 'Edutainment': workshops our Enablers present as ATMA's 'Playshops'. After all, are not most of our streetwise tips first learnt in the playgrounds of life? We might even call that not homework but homeplay, our true home being the heart not the head!

Plato said we can learn more about a child by watching it play for an hour than it will ever learn from a lifetime of lectures. In relation to education, I use the word 'complementary', not 'alternative'. If any

Soul has elected to experience the old-fashioned factory system of school instruction, what karma might I collect by robbing that Soul of his chosen chain of painful experiences? Seeing education as a warm open-hearted invitation to learn ever more about love's abundance in action, rather than a cold closed-minded left-brain imperative, is to build benign bridges and not impede progress by building walls of divisive methodologies.

Given more and more children are born with an Indigo consciousness, we at ATMA relish addressing their openness to more of the inner and outer universe than perhaps had their parents. So far. I shared thinking skills with 4-year-olds up to the time they were eleven during Saturday morning classes. In that ten years they taught me so much. I remain grateful to them all, not least the little girl who refused to enter the classroom. Asked why, Rachael stated she was too busy speaking with her Angel.

We teachers left her till she herself knew it was right for her to return to my philosophy class.

The implicit spirituality of Rachael, like all happy children, was readily accepted as necessary for their fullest development. The early need for a child to seek autonomy is not neglected by adults who see keeping control of all possible aspects of youngsters in their care as unhealthy and detrimental to the child's development.

Our Saturday classes attracted parents with offspring struggling with their regular Monday to Friday teaching regime. In state schools activities that engage the imagination are still too often missing. The more sensitive child can be left feeling lost in a herd of kids inaudibly screaming for freedom till at last released by the school bell and running pell-mell into the playground, screaming with delight.

Too much sitting, head down poring over yet another worksheet can make them passive, depersonalised and despondent. If the stress in screeching teachers is all the result of a bullying system, no wonder violence, personal aggression and mental disturbances are now prevalent in all ages. And in the Autumn of 2015, the statistics indicated that there were 400,000 failed students in the poorest areas of the UK and 4 in 10 teachers had been physically assaulted by students. Yes, children are difficult to assess in any deep way. How about giving them more scope to assess themselves? (See later how Grace saved herself this way.)

HOWARD GARDENER v DANAH ZOHAR

Apparently one in three teachers suffer from mental health problems at some point (breaking-point?) in their careers. The authorities have accepted the link between the ill-effects of mental health, this bracketed with learning difficulties. How long before they also acknowledge that thousands of schoolchildren are temperamentally entirely unsuited to mental - that is, over-narrow cerebral activities imposed by an over-intellectualizing academic elite - on open-hearted learners?The result being an unnecessary expense for the taxpayers as an epidemic of the academic injured become hungry and homeless - unless already expensively housed in jails.

All of these systemic social 'failures' increasing in number well after Howard Gardener identified over 8 different learning preferences. One of the later modes acknowledged being Natural Intelligence.

Yet that number did not include Spiritual Intelligence (SI) as exploded in the writings of Danah Zohar. No wonder we at ATMA Enterprises sense the need for so much reclamation of personal power among education's varied victims of all ages and backgrounds.

For our ATMA pioneering team we now have more than a dozen different areas of learning modes to explore with willing partners.

Respecting students' different attitudes and aptitudes, a benign educational strategy engages more facets of their imagination, innate interests and skills.

My philosophy classes were devised on ageless themes like Astronomy, Animal behaviour and the human needs for free thinking as well as the need to conform and fit in. In a firm but flexible framework, each child stayed engaged through an implicit empathy with the cosmic themes on offer.

Putting heart-centred personal experiences before head-centred instructions, it was productive and revealing in not using a one-size-fits-all approach. Instead, on offer was a range of ways in which we could all link universal themes with those we see as more personal.

Yet are they not already intimately linked, anyway...?

Like each chunk of coal can become a diamond. Like zoo animals can entertain themselves with paintbrush and canvas. Like human astronauts, feet on earth's ground, who see themselves with open eyes buzzing about around far off planets.

Such examples could be seen as the urge of all Creation towards a fuller expression of every facet of its budding qualities - as above, so below; as inside, so outside.

Time for you to cogitate on your own favourite quote, preferably one you yourself devised by way of educing your best Self in ways not on offer in the general sense by the provision of the political State and its supposed requirements of us.

Let me thank Phill Jones for bringing to life for me so vividly this picture shown below:-

BUSY BEE ALPHABET

FROM GRUBS TO COLOURFUL WINGS

WITH LOVE THEIR ALPHABET SINGS

EACH BUTTERFLY'S MARK

SHOWS ALL ITS GOD SPARK

THEIR NUMBERS MUCH UPLIFT BRINGS*!*

Below is for juniors, in a multi-sensory way, to explore their ABC. Numbers in brackets indicate seven different learning modes, offering varied ways the letters of the English alphabet can be learnt. Each is supplied with a rhyming couplet. The aim is an all-embracing approach, organic and holistic, one that can become a pleasure for children, while absorbing the basic building blocks of language. At the same time, the variety of methods and the versatility encouraged, is to engage their active imagination. Nothing more exhilarating than being with children happily enjoying themselves in their learning environment.

91

Being aware of the variety of ways in which learning is imprinted, spatial awareness for instance, can be encouraged even at the sub-aural levels. How? By internalising responses. Outwardly articulated, every letter of the alphabet, no matter how pronounced, affects the physical body, all according to the pitch of the sound and its intonations. For evidence, watch iron filings dance into different formations, all according to the variety of vibrations it experiences. Iron is also found in healthy bloodstreams. What's more, current children are often hyper-sensitive. They cringe in the presence of unloving, inharmonious sounds, especially when adults shout abuse or, in any way, belittle any struggling learner.

Think back to the days when school desks were arranged in ranks, all facing the teacher's blackboard. It was found that students given the freedom to sit where they liked, those with a willingness to help in practical ways sat nearest the teacher. These hands-on helpers seemed to learn best when involved with kinaesthetic activities. While those students who liked to listen rather than to talk often aimed for the centre of the room. As for those who learnt best through their eyes, they liked to sit at the back of the class.

You might care to remember where you used to sit in classrooms and how you responded to such a sitting position. If such a place was imposed, then in that formative early stage, a significant choice was not given; control - or rather, the teacher's fear of losing control - being the presiding imperative. Yet, as Plato inferred, so much more can be gleaned as to the true nature of each unique child by letting them make certain choices. By this means, many more social skills can be exercised and, importantly, enjoyed.

Count up how much goodwill and bonding can occur when such logistics are negotiated with all involved. Time is not wasted when a loving approach overrides all other considerations. Far better we suggest, than engaging in curricula that encourage uniformed outcomes, all over-stewed and tasteless as in a pressure-cooker. Increasingly though, customers are buying wonky veg. Yes, they may all get boxed up together but the discerning consumer prefers a carrot with character. Meanwhile, the bait swallowed by most parents is that excellent exam passes ensure a successful future with, down the time-line, no mid-life crisis 'necessary' in later life.

However, school regimes are spiked, rather than spiced, with the fears of failure of such imposed examinations. And through that stress, the fears of being different and not fitting in, greatly add to the all-round distress. This drive towards uniformed standards for children and teachers leads to more absenteeism and illness; all prevailing ailments like depression and acts of self-harming are preventable.

This illustration by Sara Olpin. An ex-pupil of mine she agreed to illustrate my second Talking book, BRIGHT EYES AND BUBBLES,

Happiness is healthy*!*

Consider this quote from one of the ATMA Team:

'Grades and intelligence don't really have much to do with each other.....It's a shame children's feeling of self-worth is determined by a child's ability memorize, repeat, and obey...Intelligence goes FAR beyond educational institutions.' So says ATMA Enabler, Hilary Newhall.

Hidden Masters of the Ancient Wisdom would agree with Hilary. Systems of faith based on fanatical attachments to selected dogmas, because not holistic, will most likely end in emotional fundamentalism and spawn even more frayed nerves. Yet historically, all great spiritual teachers - like some modern physicists - indicate there is an abundance of all-embracing but dispassionate love for all life forms.

This is nurtured through our working playfully on the inner person and its needs and, by this, exploring each individual's fullest potential.

Hence, we at ATMA claim that the most effective examination for life-long nourishment is Self-Examination. To paraphrase Socrates,

'An unexamined life is not worth living - unless to its full potential.' As if the populace sensed the value of this truism, no wonder that in 2013 the word SELFIE was chosen as the Word of the Year by the Oxford English Dictionary.

Since then international city banks, thanks to a software package called Perceive, Selfies are being used by way of biometrics versification customers' identity. But a photographic profile linked to social media, is but a superficial reading of the real inner person.

Despite these advance algorithms being able to detect the difference between looking at a real person and a photograph, in the year 2015, 5.1 million financial frauds were detected. To some extent, after all, aren't all identities 'imagined'?

Allowing that those still resisting total Self-knowledge, are capable of, yes, self-deception, that is why Bow Focske, presenting her skills under the business title No Frills Well-Being, inaugurated a Part Two to our probing Self-identifying profiles. Please engage with both parts of MINING ME on our ATMA website. Those who have done it more than once have found it a useful toolkit for cumulative data collating on their evolving Self. The white working class child can more quickly find this mode of Self-detection revealing maybe than those nervous of introspection because of prior-conditioning.

Meanwhile, half the recruits selected by big business companies use a variety of personality testing, including psychometric testing, before employing youngsters; the majority of the brightest brains having come from independent schools or grammar schools. Traditionally, the more academic educational establishments - less so now, perhaps - encouraged free-thinkers through 'character' training. We consider the true character is determined more by awareness and consciousness at work and play, rather than by any IQ tests, some now over a hundred years old!

Appropriately, now let's introduce you to our way of not so much teaching, but allowing the building blocks of language to become at best a transformative learning experience. I won't sulk if you decide to skip on to other pages more suited to your prevailing interests!

With the BUSY BEE ABC, as with the exercises that follow, we would ask that there is enough creative flexibility to include the pupils' suggestions and, where suitable, their individual responses to the stimuli to be acknowledged, not rejected as inconvenient. Such impulses can be weaved into repeatable and enjoyable learning rituals. And grateful for their help, let's supplement students' suggestions with multi-media back-ups. Even without the latest computers, these can include mobiles; PowerPoint, flash cards, music and video footage of earlier classes to show them their improvements. Such visual and aural aides can help most learners memorise more effectively.

Research suggests that most of us learn quickest by emotional associations and by enjoyable repetition. Kindly note, however, that the numbers shown in brackets for suggested learning modes are only examples. Human potential being so versatile, and the brain so pliable, no learner should feel constrained by any one suggested system.

Many of the items given below can become even more inter-curricula. For example, bees traditionally were seen as insect Angels and as such, they are 'Little servants of God that originated in Paradise'. Hence healthy flora, fruit and harvests bringing heaven to earth. With bees above blooms fertilising our fields and gardens, the need below is the nourishment that rainwater brings. It is the grayling fish in rivers, lakes and canals that show where water is still pure enough for human consumption.

How long before the inspectors of Ofsted are blessed with similar virtues. All further contributions and activities to the BUSY BEE ABC are welcomed! But whatever else, delight in the process of this energising matrix of exercises.

Just to repeat, the numbers below in brackets represent the seven learning modes as demonstrated, and more fully explored in ATMA's MASTER LEARNING MENU explained later.

While it is true that all the numbers represent only the author's suggestions, no hard and fast rules should apply. Allow for human variables.

Yes, let all choices be negotiated with teachers, parents and of course, the children themselves, incrementally. Important that pupils can grow confident in their own ability to contribute creative choices without criticism. This will help them to share cooperatively.

Sometime in pairs role-playing can be offered. That is, children taking turns to act as 'teacher' and 'pupil' and then, possibly reversing roles. At all ages, best we teach what we ourselves most need to learn - both sides of all wide open, not closed, doors! As imagination is activated in this multi-sensory, integrated series of activities, may they open not just the dictionary wider but the whole universe of learning.

As for our code, the numbers 1 to 7 represent one of the seven main learning aptitudes as listed below. These are appended at the end of each sentence within the BUSY BEE ABC; that is, appearing after each rhyming couplet.

1. Musical - sensitivity to sounds, inner and outer;

2. Intrapersonal-transcendent insights, a sense of Soul;

3. Interpersonal - social skills, cooperative;

4. Logical – deductive thinking skills;

5. Visual - spatial perceptions, colour sensitive;

6. Verbal - linguistic skills, mentally mercurial;

7. Bodily - hands on, practical and constructive,

Visually, within each group of four rhyming sentences flashed onto a screen, the letters being learnt are shown in BOLD type.

All of these, and other empowering approaches, can be used to repeat necessary learning without, hopefully, too much tedium.

Over all, llet controversial modalities, fearlessly encourage VARIETY of approach! Creative engagement always generates energy!

Throughout, identify which modes most develop children with a central word for education - ENTHUSIASM!

These are the unforgettable learning moments at work as in PLAY stretching young minds and muscles in happy activities!

HAPPY TEACHERS – HAPPY CHILDREN!

BUSY-BEE ABC

A is for ants so easy to say. (3, 6, 7 - oral, pair work?)

B is for bees all busy at play. (1,5, 6 - buzzing dance?)

C is for black cats that can jump on a wall. (1, 5, 7 - mime & music?)

And now with **ABC** we **c**an all pl**a**y **ba**ll – **c**atch!.**(**1, 4, 5, 7 - active memory games?)

D is for dogs that love digging up bones. (1, 5, 7 - fossil hunting, pictures?)

E is for elephants that love lifting stones. (1,2,7 - design & Technology, Brain Gym?)

F is for friends that have fun jumping high. (1, 2, 4 - mathematical games?)

DEF Dr**e**am Ang**e**ls h**e**lp **f**airi**e**s to **f**ly. (1, 3, 4, 5 - spiritual, paintings, stories?)

G is for goats chewing granny's green coats. (1, 6, 7 - mime, cartoons?)

H is for horses heard sniffing hard oats. (1, 4, 5 - history, husbandry?)

I is for inches, me standing up TALL! (1, 2, 3, + hugs and cheers!)

GHI It's **g**ood to sing **high** one song with all. (1, 4, 5, 3 - choir music?)

J is for juices and fruit jellies from trees. (3, 6, 7 - ecology?)

K is for kangaroos king penguins that freeze. (1, 4, 7, - mime, geographic pictures?)

L is for lazy lizards that lie in the lovely sun. (1, 3, 4 - science, astronomy?)

JKL Keen **k**nowing **l**etters is **j**olly **l**ovely good fun! (1, 4, 7, 6 - free expression?)

M is for mother and me her good child. (1, 3, 4 - role-play babyhood?)

N is for naught never naughty and wild. (1, 2, 7 - mime naught, picture of same?)

O is all round like a hole in the air. (1, 2, 7 - show halo and/or ozone layer?)

MNO mum and **m**e **n**eed **o**ur **o**wn teddy-bear. (1, 4, 6, 2 - nature studies, cuddles?)

P is for pussy-cats that play with pet mice. (1, 3, 4 - food-chain, pet care?)

Q is for quartz crystals and queens' quiet advice. (3, 6, 5 - social history, healing?)

R is for rabbits in round holes around roads. (1, 2, 7 - country pictures, safety drills?)

PQR Pairs of **r**abbits can **q**uickly jum**p** **p**ast **r**ound toads. (1, 4, 7, 2 - threatened species?)

S is for salt and sugar found in fat dogs. (1, 3, 4 - muscle testing, energy awareness?)

T is thin tadpoles turning into fat frogs. (1, 3, 7 - evolution, video, transformation?)

U under my umbrella no sun my wet hair dries.

STU see **s**hining **st**ar**s** **u**nderneat**h** my **shut** eye**s**. (7, 3, 6, 4 visions, rainbow colours?)

V is for vegetables very tasty and green. (2, 3, 7 - gardening, health, food miles?)

W is for water to wash us all clean. (1, 3, 7 - plumbing, amenities, hygiene?)

X is for extra trees now and for extra fresh air. (1, 2, 7 - name games on nature rambles?)

VWX **v**ery e**x**pressive **v**oices sing every**w**here. (2, 3, 5, 6 - E**x**pand my heart', freestyle? Enjoy e**v**eryone's smile!)

Y is for yoga, **y**our young fists open wide (1, 2, 7 - body stretching, relaxing?)

Z is for **z**ebras snoring side by side (3, 5, 7 - dreams, pictures?)

YZ my last two letters to learn today (1, 5, 7 - sign-language, memory training?)

YZ Though we're **y**oung all **z**ing and shout out HU-RAY! (4, 5, 7, 1 - oral/aural celebrations!

Who qualifies as an INDIGO? Is your answer the same as ours? If so, you should enjoy exploring the next chapter. It starts with an INDIGO ALPHABET, that leading into the research details of MY IDENTITY AUDIT.

5 THE INDIGO ALPHABET

The genetic alphabet talks

As individualised as walks

Each letter of law Miracles ignore

Freewill reigns at all our roads' forks

I can only guess at your opinions so far. How much at variance might they be from what here is being proposed? By exploring your own views, I now invite you to scan our Indigo Alphabet below.

A 'rose my any other name would smell as sweet!' The press have dubbed these folks 'Generation 'X'. Others choose the adjective Star and Rainbow, whereas Jane Lloyd uses the term Orchid. TV commenters have claimed, whatever they're called, they are 'hard to read and harder to understand'.

Like you and me? Or not?

Choose say, three letters. These could be the initials of your name. Mine are COG. The qualities starting with these letters really do reflect my current character. Below are just suggestions; hence the cop-out questions-marks! On your voyage of Self-discovery, enjoy the journey!

INDIGO ALPHABET

AWARENESS? **A**DVENTUROUS? **A**DHD? **A**RROGANT? **A**LTRUISITIC?

BOSSY? **B**EAUTIFUL? FEELS **B**LESSED? **B**OUNTERFUL?

CREATIVE? **C**URIOUS? **C**OSMIC **C**ONSCIOUSNESS? **C**ARING?

DIVINE? **D**EPRESSIVE? **D**IFFERENT? **D**ISCERNER? **D**AYDREAMER?

EMPHATIC? **E**LITIST? WEEPS **E**ASILY? **E**NERGETIC?

FAR-SIGHTED? **F**RIENDS WITH OLDER FOLKS? OFTEN **F**RUSTRTED?

GULLIBLE, **G**NOSTIC GOD-BOTHERER? **G**ENEROUS?

HATES REPETITIVE OCCUPATIONS? INWARDLY **H**ARDY? **H**EALER?

IMAGINATIVE? **I**NTUITIVE? **I**NNOVATOR? WANTS TO **I**MPROVE LIFE?

JUDGEMENTAL? - SEES 'JUSTICE' AS KARMA'S **J**UST EQUATIONS?

KNOWING - YET SUSPICIOUS OF '**K**NOWLEDGE'? **K**INDLY?

LONESOME? **L**OVING? SOMETIMES FEELING **L**OST?

MILD-MANNERED? **M**ODEST? **M**ISUNDERSTOOD?

NEW AGE **N**OVELTY PIONEER? **N**EUROTIC?

OUT OF THE ORDINARY? **O**UT-OF-BODY OPERATOR? **O**CCULIST?

PERSONLY **P**ERCEPTIVE? **P**RECOCIOUS? **P**SYCHIC. **P**ATRONISING?

QUEEN/KING-LIKE? **Q**UAINT? **Q**UALLSOME? OPEN TO **Q**UALMS

RULE-CHALLENGER? **R**EBELLIOUS? CAN BE UN**R**ELIABLE?

SOLITARY? **S**CHOOL-PHOBIC? **S**INCERE? **S**ELFIE-DEVELOPMENTAL?

TOUCHY-FEELY? **T**ACTILE? EASILY FEELS **T**RAPPED?

UNIQUE? **U**SEFUL TO THE **U**NFOLDMENT OF **U**NUSUAL IDEAS?

VAIN?   SEEMINGLY   **V**AGUE?   AND/OR   **V**OLATILE   AND **V**ERSATILE?

WORKAHOLIC? CAPABLE OF **W**ONDER? **W**ILLFUL? **W**ISE?

X-RAY VISIONARY?

YEARNING? STAYS **Y**OUNG LOOKING AND AT HEART?

ZIKAR - SENSITIVELY RESPONSIVE TO SOUNDS AS MANTRAS?

Did you enjoy exploring that? It can be a playful way of sharing with friends·

If so, you might like to visit www.atmaenterprises.co.uk and consider being part of our survey. No pressure, of course.

Maybe AGAIN since we can never stop discovering MORE about our potential POWERS, on our home page, are two versions of MINING ME.

We all have hidden treasures to harvest and most of them could benefit from being brought into the daylight and polished more brightly.

To supplement your personal researches please listen to ATMA's MP3 *Joyful Gemstones.* Others in that series of TEMPLE TAPES, is *Money as a Mantra* and *Thinking Well with Tinnitus and Dr. HU.*

I wonder to what degree your inner gifts and interests were recognised, let alone nourished, by your childhood teachers.

What follows shortly is a report on MY IDENTITY AUDIT (MIA). It evolved during the time of an earlier incarnation of ATMA. That was INaSENSE, inaugurated by Susan Wilmot-Josife.

It is included here because we still think it resonates with the present aims of ATMA Enterprises. Please see if you agree.

Apart from that, Susan's struggles with education on behalf of her three children featured fully in my book, FREE SCHOOLS??? - That's the Spirit! (Pegasus, Vanguard Press 2000.)

MY IDENTITY AUDIT (MIA)

This survey was conducted with over two hundred year-ten schoolchildren in the North of England. Ninety-eight questions invited participants to mark out of seven (7 is always top mark) a range of person-centred and probing questions; everything from WHERE DO I COME FROM? to HOW MUCH DO YOU VALUE YOUR SENSES?

The motive to formulate this survey came from my years teaching in comprehensive schools. With some dismay I watched keen youngsters become too unthinkingly compliant; growing up round-shouldered, bug-eyed and with little clue as to who they are or why; with a limited sense of Self and their inner riches. Secular cynicism too often becomes the diminishing result of such a diminishing system. Instead that is, of nurturing a healthy scepticism, one that can lead to Self-motivated and Self-accepted inner certainties; well, enough meanwhile to instil an inner sense of security.

A waiver: unlike political polls! With MIA, no proselytizing took place prior to these youngsters being invited to contribute to this survey. While a number of schools had several nudges before the tutors found time for the questionnaire to be to filled in, no complaints were received. Plus at least one significant compliment. That came from the headteacher who said that MIA made a useful supplementary part of the students' learning kit.

Having taught all ages, I had privately felt that such a survey could fruitfully be employed by much younger pupils. See how much wisdom lies latent in children as described in *Soul Centred Education* (Third edition, CompletelyNovel 2014). But do controlling adults fear their children's free-flowing insights? To quote from my Soul book, 'From Satan's stable, fear is the dark stalking horse. Corrosive feelings of fear and helplessness can block our ability to to believe in magic, miracles and in the marvel of ME'.

Yes, it could be claimed that pupil time with their class teacher could well be amplified to everybody's advantage by accepting such exercises. It's people with undiscovered qualities who need educating, rather than being delivered yet more draconian policies that crush a person-centred approach. Yet a diagnostic toolkit is not popular with those who profit from society's ills, in or out of the National Health Service; despite the fact, 'Prevention is cheaper than cure.' And for us all, the earlier the better!

Surprises awaited us. Was MY IDENTITY AUDIT too late for our teenage clients to reclaim some Self-esteem? Yet in the main, these soon-to-be school leavers highly rated aspects of existence not experienced in most classrooms. Co-incidentally, Amanda Spielman I watched on TV being questioned about her possible role as a new boss of Ofsted. She said what goes on in classrooms was central in her concerns. Note, not what goes on in the heart and mind of people, big or small, be they students, teachers or indeed parents.

As for INaSENSE, the third set of seven questions related to, not five, but six senses. The aim was for them to appreciate the differences in learning styles and, by that, to prioritise their own preferred modes of learning. In the list we included common sense as well as the other five senses. In those times of risk aversion, it was interesting for us to see if teachers' taboo on TOUCH had any impact on the scores the teenagers awarded themselves. After all, schoolchildren must have witnessed injured kids crying and watched as no adult was 'allowed' to handle them on pain or being accused of being a 'perve'. One teacher threatened in a volatile school yard punch-up, was told, 'No blood, don't get involved.'

Corporal punishment was banned in UK schools as late as 1999 and currently would not be necessary in a benign education setting (See Finnish Lessons by Pasi Sahlberg)

Yet sadly there is at least one Hindu Nationalist school in India where the teachers carry sticks. Reportedly, interviewed students say they put up with the beatings in order to get good qualifications. Contrast that with one 12-year boy in England who said, "We kids don't stop learning but somehow schools manage it.' Contrast that with Kenya where on the day of writing this, 98 schools had been set alight.

In systems in which stress seems all but mandatory, how dehumanising are directives that are based, no matter how subtly, on coercion? Yet, although dismayed by such demands, how many tender-hearted teachers rebel? I'm advised that it depends on the school but that some enlightened folks do ensure children are cared for properly i.e. cuddled - appropriately etc - it's a matter of having sensible policies and approaches as well as trusting the teachers to enjoy knowing the children in their charge.

Thanks to David Renner, the results of the INaSENSE survey you now have the chance to scrutinise. But before I give the result of the MY IDENTITY AUDIT, another anecdote taken from a primary classroom. The teacher asked the class of over thirty what is the most important word in the dictionary. Several hands were raised but the girl who looked as if she might burst if not chosen to speak, when asked, pointing at her heart and said, "I, Miss!"

"But Pat, I, that is such a small word."

"I know, Miss, that's how you make us feel, Miss. Small."

I include this here because in seven questions posed on the human senses, the word - indeed the quality - that most of our Year Ten students chose as top priority also started with the letter 'I'. When addressing a group of educated adults in a Mind! Body! Spirit! event organised by Rosemary Douglas, I solicited answers to the self-same question; namely, what human gift did these youngsters choose as the most important?

It took eight guesses, ranging from Information to Intelligence, before one lady at the back with her hand in the air gave the right answer. Guess now what these young adults chose as their necessary chief sense, one not featured or facilitated in top-down, mug-an'-jug teaching methods to which they had been subjected? The answer can be found in the data given below. But first, a reminder.

This early version of MY IDENTITY AUDIT was conducted over a decade ago. It covered over 200 near-adults about to go to colleges. The students had no contact with the compilers of this person-probing profile so we can safely claim that, unlike political polls, no lobbying before the event took place. No reports of spoilt papers (!) and that only one headteacher gave an opinion. That was based on his own volunteered participation. Remember, he agreed with us that it was a useful teaching tool.

I wonder if you will be as amazed by these results as were we. Compare their answers with the fodder served up to them to regurgitate in examinations, most of the content unrelated to the immediate person-centred needs of students.

Hence, classroom 'facts' will likely get forgotten by the time they fall in love.

Better still if they quickly regain their love of learning more about life and indeed, more about the qualities of of life-enhancing love itself.

Now for some results to a selection of areas covered:

1. WHAT DRIVES ME?

2. WHAT SHAPES ME?

3. HOW MUCH DO I VALUE MY SENSES?

4. WHERE DO I COME FROM?

5. WHAT INSIGHTS MAKE ME MORE REAL?

6. WHAT MOST INSPIRES ME?

7. WHAT MOST INTERESTS ME?

See chart on the next page, please.

While it is only a small section of the fully survey, the flavour of it we hope you will be able to savour - if not dribble!

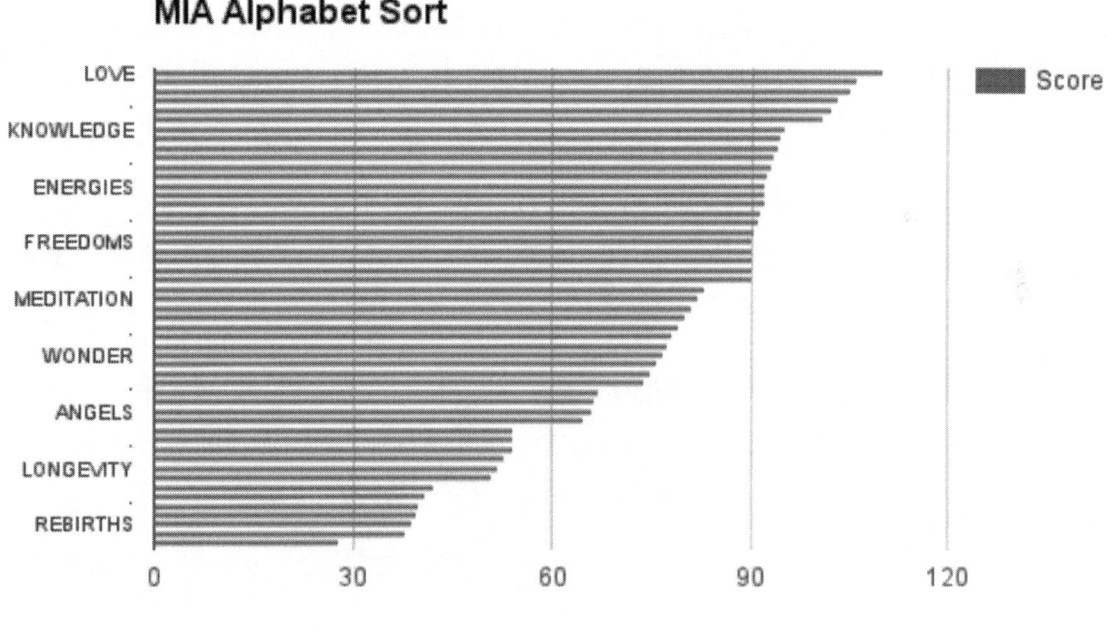

MIA Alphabet Sort

Number of Ticks

ZIKARS?

As a precursor to the Indigo Alphabet in this book, I wrote a similar list of 26 words for our applicants to consider. That was given at the end of INaSENSE by way of inviting a greater expansion of Self-awareness. Well, to find a suitable word starting with the letter X was tricky, given that xenophobia was best kept out of bounds. But what about the last letter of our alphabet? I came up with the word ZIKAR. Indeed, you might have noticed it in The Indigo Alphabet above and wondered about its inclusion. Some students managed to grade such a word, a word they were unlikely to have understood. Were the grades chosen based on their conditioned reflex to stay obedient to authority as in school exams? Better to give even a wrong answer than to leave it blank? Might get a mark for trying, eh? So in revised versions of MIA, we replaced 'Zikar' with 'Zombies'.

Encouraged by us, senior students produced their own 3Rs – These we read as - **R**ecognition! **R**elevance! **R**ealisations! Might these choices of theirs show some intuition? Such as...

The Rights of Man as part of God's plan

Allow us to do everything we can

As Cause and effect

We reap each defect

To balance all try a Soul scan?

6 MAKING A BETTER ME

"My tummy fill and make me fat*!*"

The purring heard is Felix Cat·

"Now please Mouse don't squeal,"

Said Cat, "You're my meal,

"No time to play or have a chat·"

By way of a complementary stimulus, for the hungry learner, try offering a menu of fables for them to feast upon.   These can add spicy flavour to the more stale but necessary fodder provided. No better delight than to steer each student into the wonders of being ME! Interesting to note though, that in asking schoolchildren to cogitate on what aspects of human nature they themselves can 'Make ME' more fulfilled, the very phrase 'MAKE me' remains ambivalent.

Think of 'The teachers make me sit still in a stuffy classroom when I'd rather get out of maths and play football with me mates'. In one large drama studio I did not need to teach those young teens the word xenophobia. Spending voluntary time in my studio during lunch breaks, they unselfconsciously welcomed the refugee children who had recently joined us. With them, all playing indoor football, the foreign children learnt English phrases far quicker than in my English classes when forced to sit still and concentrate and grow fat. If it had not been an Inner City location, I'd have had them all out-of-doors, of course.

GIVE ME YOUR ANSWER DO

In My Identity Audit, a section called MY ALTERNATIVES was offered. This invitation to contribute appears also in ATMA's MINING ME. Did you relish the three highest scores shown at the top of the bar chart above? 'Love' was their top requirement. As a middle-aged student teacher, I deliberately searched dozens of books on education. I could not find the word LOVE anywhere. Eventually, instead I found the word 'happiness' - in American publications.

That was before an explosion of campus killings; students 'Happy' by Right of the Constitution to carry a gun - like toy ones for British toddlers? - in order to shoot fellow scholars and their teachers. Still, the Indigo born with cosmic consciousness, soon works out that this is a warring planet. By struggling with binary polarities, like us all, Indigos can often hone their abilities to make choices that enhance and enrich their better nature.

For evidence, we offer our ATMA team, many of whom, as late developers, have all had transformative experiences. A central aim we share is to guide others to their life-improving epiphanies; each to bloom more beautifully in their own chosen way. Even a back garden in a council house can be made a tiny paradise on earth.

The humble daisy flower, with its sunny centre, represents cosmic consciousness. The stakes are higher after death as we graduate to finer teachings. Hence the phrase, 'Pushing UP the daisies'. As for making choices on earth, it is not like standing on a see-saw? Our wobbling selves have yet to find the the Middle Way, the neutral fulcrum between alternative ends. Options accepted freely, without duress or stress, will always be more personally rewarding than when obeying disagreeable orders.

Ageless Indigos are natural entrepreneurs. As such, they are nobody's mindless serf. Unlike computerised humanoids that fall over. So far as I know, these can't yet pick themselves up. Unlike the Indigo child. Indigos quickly grasp the importance of making their own choices in life. In making such choices between, say, listening inwards more than outwards; following the teachings of the Light instead of the dark; putting themselves UP rather than letting others push them down, they survive more fruitfully. Yes, the mature Indigos aim to take responsibility for all they are and do. No wonder they can be seen as odd misfits. Thus sadly, the more fragile ones can suffer from self-punishment. Like those who cut themselves to prove they are for real by making their pain as vivid and immediate as flowing blood. Theirs.

As for Indigo parents, playfully they can say Upsey-daisy when picking up a fallen child; or if the kid falls again, 'Oopsey-daisy!' This introduces what I call the 'Careful, or you'll fall' syndrome. It goes like this. Picture an Indigo child running along a high wall. What might an Indigo adult shout out? Might their chosen words be, 'Careful darling, or you'll fall!'? Out of those five words, did the emotional tone of voice seem overly directive? For the child trained to be obedient, might he or she 'permit' to become indelibly imprinted by the word FALL, rather than by the word 'darling'? And then, that child, trained to follow 'instructions', could lose balance and fall to the ground.

Both in shock, the distressed adult, in picking up the young injured body, would blame the kid for being so stupid. Like many abused victims, such a child might indeed accept the parent's verdict and, feeling guilty, start to close down the gleeful and adventurous spirit that so excited the impulse to climb onto the wall. Result? Was this situation what both adult and child 'deserved'? For both of them, did it 'Serve them right'?

BEST SUITED

In these end times of muddled morals, as if today's legislators and journalists are all agnostics, they wield emotive words and phrases like, 'These INNOCENT victims DESERVE better than that.' Or again, 'It's their RIGHT to ask for higher wages; but the RIGHT of the bosses to say, 'That's right. My workers don't DESERVE more than a zero hours contract.' And for the servile, the usual get-out clause states, 'I did not make the rules.' Inwardly or outwardly, these cliches get challenged by the Indigos. RIGHTly so? Dear reader, your call. But if you are sufficiently comfortable, let alone curious, to read on, later let's challenge the idea that we are never truly INNOCENT, not spiritually. Or ignorant. Not really.

This accepted as possibly true, in the age-old struggles between love and power, enlightened Indigos will never allow themselves to stay a victim. Hence the growing numbers of school phobics of all ages, and their spin-off, Home Educators. And this singularity of approach might be said to be widely reflected in the number of singletons now, be they single parents (two million one parent families as well as thirty-seven and a half thousand children educated at home); or loners of all kinds and of all ages. Feeling isolated, how many resist peer pressure and do not risk cyber bullying by using social media? When I was a troubled teen I used to have secret assignations, but at least they were face to face; albeit one of us risking a slap on one cheek or another!

I wrote the above on the morning of Wednesday, 16th September, 2015. The BBC news that morning reported that 1 in 6 Secondary schools and 1 in 4 schools inspected by Ofsted were rated as inadequate. Further, that in the Autumn scramble to get children into the 'best' schools, those schools that parents felt best suited their child's future prospects. In this quest, 50,000 families failed.

'Best suited'? In our Sunday best or birthday suit? On my 21st birthday my parents gave me a smart present; smart because it suited the fashion of the day. Behold, I unpacked not one, but two, hideous Sunday best suits. Both were striped and, to me, suffocatingly double-breasted. One was an institutional brown, as if from some Edwardian smoking-room; the other a dull smokey blue and just as striped. How much gratitude this ungrateful brat simulated, I can't recall. My parents' good intentions, like most birthday presents, suited the taste of the giver rather than the receiver.

Yes, the head of the family wanted his first son to appear dressed like his dear papa. Just as school uniforms insist on short back and sides like the army and all in the same uniform. And that assumed need for cloning, a system that suits those who'd cling to control over their troops, this is exactly what leads to a confusing sterilising standardisation with conformist standards imposed.

Mavericks unite, OK?

Never mind love as an educational ideal. What about simple kindness? Would it not have been kinder to have asked me whether or not I felt good in a mud-coloured suit? Instead, they could have sent the money saved - not the awful suits - to the Jesuit Missionaries in native Africa. I jest, of course. But how much pain, stress and downright hypocritical compliance could be saved with more honest consultations?

Good manners can be so hollow. Yes, consult the children more. It's their body they need to keep healthy; their heart they're best keeping open to more love and blessings; their mind they best keep sane. In short, we at ATMA see the need for radical reforms for society at large. All of these complementary strategies, be they preventative - our preferred option - or remedial, start with the wish to develop to optimum effectiveness; for each person to lead a life that best suits their unique individuality. As Aristotle knew, 'Educating the head without educating the heart, is no education at all'. ATMA includes educating the spirit also. Why?

Because -

Sacred ignorance is illusion

It invites psychic intrusion

Life's fruits we all earn

As love's laws we discern

Concord our karmic conclusion

INNOCENCE - A MYTH?

As I write, a ten-year report has just been completed. It's title is INTERNATIONAL HAPPINESS: A New View on the Measure of Performance. It's an inte-disciplinary international survey. What you might see as significant is that the compilers found that human happiness does not seem to increase with economic growth. It measured the happiness quotient of children in a cross section of countries. England, despite boasts of the Big Society, came near to the bottom of the list; behind Ethiopia, that country then between countrywide droughts.

Ethiopia? The third world country where in the 1980's widespread famine haunted the indigenous residents? Where the parents of many rural children cannot now afford to send their wage earning offspring to school? But so fitting the philosophy of our ATMA remit, another timely survey illustrates aspects of the human capacity for inner knowing driven by curiosity. Such qualities, mostly ignored in Western modes of education, are nonetheless already innate in us before adult instructions are all but enforced.

To surprise illiterate village children, cardboard boxes were left seemingly unattended. Inside, firmly sealed up, were laptops. Yet one peasant boy not only ripped off the tape (a sticky job) but also found the on/off switch, the like of which this lifetime he had never seen before; let alone any other form of technology. It took him four minutes. With other children their 'expertise' did not stop there.

Within five days they were using 47 apps per child per day. All this remember without a teacher. Before two weeks, these village youngsters were singing ABC songs in English. Within five months they had hacked Android. Some educated idiot, maybe in the organisation's Media Lab, had disabled the camera. But the children - brought up with no street signs, newspapers or packaged food - figured out each laptop had a camera, hacking activities being the amazing result of their inquisitive investigations.

What does this signify to our so-called civilised Western mind? What about the ever ageless controversy about the comparative effectiveness of nature V nurture? These days British children brought up with YouTube and game consoles love their iPad more than their schoolteachers? Or take the case of the ten-year-old musical composer prodigy, multi-talented and home-educated Alma Deutscher. Her favourite teachers are her violin and piano; she now a concert soloist as well as a singer of arias taken from her own opera, the first being written when she was four. Indeed, a modern day Mozart.

The ageless Indigo consciousness is not to do with cognitive intelligence but more a matter of innate awareness, this informed by centuries of many varied experiences on earth?

Discuss?

iPLAYERS IN COSMIC CLASSROOMS

When I worked with Susan Wilmot Joseph, a single mother of three, she had become greatly disillusioned by the educational regimes in both state and public schools. Her three unhappy but gifted children were not been catered for as unique individuals with special requirements, spiritually, emotionally or socially. I had taught all three on Saturday mornings before they entered Secondary schools and before they got closed down by depression. No wonder in Britain mental disturbances are alarmingly on the increase when most of the prescribed curricula are too MENTAL, and too left brain at that. No surprise then that those who can't cope become 'unbalanced'?

It's over twenty years since I retired from classroom teaching. What with Academies and Free Schools how much has improved? To find out I met a lady who got sacked from a local Secondary School. Why? For giving unhappy children - more often roving the corridors - rather than sat bowed down in rows being 'subjugated' by stressed-out schoolteachers anxiously clinging onto their mortgages.

One anecdote told me how much things had changed - for the worse. It concerns a support teacher we'll call Julie. Trying to coax runaway pupils back into classrooms despite her wish to give these children the individual attention they craved, one teenager we'll call Jake was banging his head against the corridor wall. When asked to

126

explain himself, Jake eventually told Julie, "They just don't get me, Miss..."

Given the pain he was suffering, it would be too easy, indeed patronising, for Julie to say to Jake, "Boy, it is YOUR karmic job to get YOU!" If only Jake could have been confident enough to repost, "GET YOU, Miss!" Yet, after years of being conditioned to shut up, know nothing until instructed; to stay uncomplainingly obedient to those who KNOW what Jake needs, all of this is surely a recipe for some kind of sickness.

Does too much time staring at electronic screens lead to sickness? Is injurious to the development of the brain and, educationally, result in a restless spirit and a low boredom threshold? One computer programmer stated that the parents of some of the leading lights in the world of screen technology, as in social media, forbid their children to use screens until they are older. ATMA's David Renner suggests this danger might well be reduced. How?

By a wider use of the black screen. This will minimise the constant glare and save precious young learners from light pollution.

UNEXPECTED SURPRISE

Dis-ease in the human spirit we can see by inspecting the records of school attendance. In the year my book on Free Schools appeared, 57 million days of school days were missed by truants. By 2015, 12,479 people were found guilty of truancy offences, up by

22%; add 9,214 fines, averaging £172, issued to adilts. As for loving parents on a limited income, those who took their children on holiday during term time, 20,000 truancy fines went unpaid. My grandmother used to say, 'Travel broadens the mind.'

Wife of gold and silversmith Omar Ramsden, my well-travelled grandmother, died alienating herself from her daughter, my mother. In the case of my years of grieving after the death of my grandma, I believed in asking the ever-alert 'Upstairs' to let me have contact with her, myself if not her, believing in the indestructibility of Soul. Yet for years, no communication, despite pleas from various clairvoyants. I needed to rid myself of growing doubts; in short, I had to learn to 'let go and let God'. It worked! I believe it always will for every single seeker, just so long as they harmonise with the loving Laws of Creation. To my 'unexpected' astonishment - Grandma always was theatrical – she appeared in a dream. Epic double-doors, studded with opals and other jewels, with a stately pace, slowly opened towards me. Was a departed member of some Royal Family about to enter? A suitable thought, since Ann Ramsden had been famous as the Queen of amateur Shakespeare amongst London's glittering literati.

Swanning majestically into view, she came to a halt. In an imperious pose. Ample bosom held high, she proclaimed, 'Whoever would have thought the universe had so much to teach one?'

Then vanished*!*

Another confirmation for me that the 'invisible' agencies of Spirit have far superior teachers than any schoolteacher on earth. Hence, the importance of imagination. No longer an angry Roman Catholic, or even a resentful lapsed one, I can now thank those 'universal' teachings' for enlivening my early imagination with stories of amazing miracles like petals falling from the sky and moving statues of the Virgin Mary while others were weeping over the evil doings of mankind.

Not just the Indigo students respond to so-called fairy stories, but so in their own way will every child. No wonder Snow White and its like are evergreen classics.

The 'mythical consciousness' written about by Joel Goldsmith is a part of the human condition. For optimum spiritual health it is necessary to keep a clear wariness of the more dubious psychic energies and their possibly malign entities. These emanate from the realms above the apparent binding binaries of past and present; up and down; in, out and all other dualities. Hence, a degree of uncertainty.

Double checking all guidance is a good tip in order to prevent debilitating deceptions.

How is is possible for every Indigo student to utilise their chief gift; to develop that with passion and enjoy life more on their own terms? That is made possible by each learner in turn keeping faithful to their life's mission. This requires a sustained and determined effort to fully discover, define, and then develop, the spiritual side of the true Self, SOUL. Whoever said reincarnation was easy...what with no Soul born innocent given backpacks of past baggage? But the challenges can become exhilarating!

Why not engage with ATMA's 7 course 'meal' called MY MASTER LEARNING MENU (MMLM)? As with Mining Me, the 'meat' of the 7 nourishing courses is MY MISSION ON EARTH.   All displayed below are awaiting invitations.

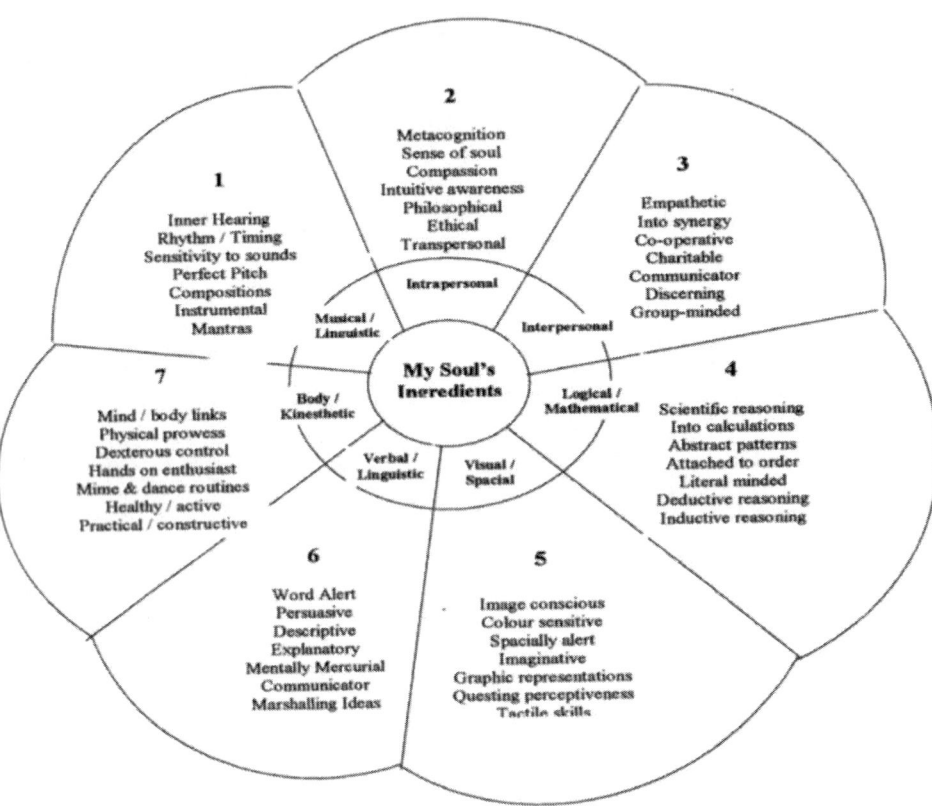

2

Metacognition
Sense of soul
Compassion
Intuitive awareness
Philosophical
Ethical
Transpersonal

1

Inner Hearing
Rhythm / Timing
Sensitivity to sounds
Perfect Pitch
Compositions
Instrumental
Mantras

3

Empathetic
Into synergy
Co-operative
Charitable
Communicator
Discerning
Group-minded

Intrapersonal

Musical /
Linguistic

Interpersonal

**My Soul's
Ingredients**

7

Mind / body links
Physical prowess
Dexterous control
Hands on enthusiast
Mime & dance routines
Healthy / active
Practical / constructive

Body /
Kinesthetic

Logical /
Mathematical

4

Scientific reasoning
Into calculations
Abstract patterns
Attached to order
Literal minded
Deductive reasoning
Inductive reasoning

Verbal /
Linguistic

Visual /
Spacial

6

Word Alert
Persuasive
Descriptive
Explanatory
Mentally Mercurial
Communicator
Marshalling Ideas

5

Image conscious
Colour sensitive
Spacially alert
Imaginative
Graphic representations
Questing perceptiveness
Tactile skills

132

THE MASTER LEARNING MENU
MY CAROUSEL OF OPPORTUNITIES
FIGURE 1

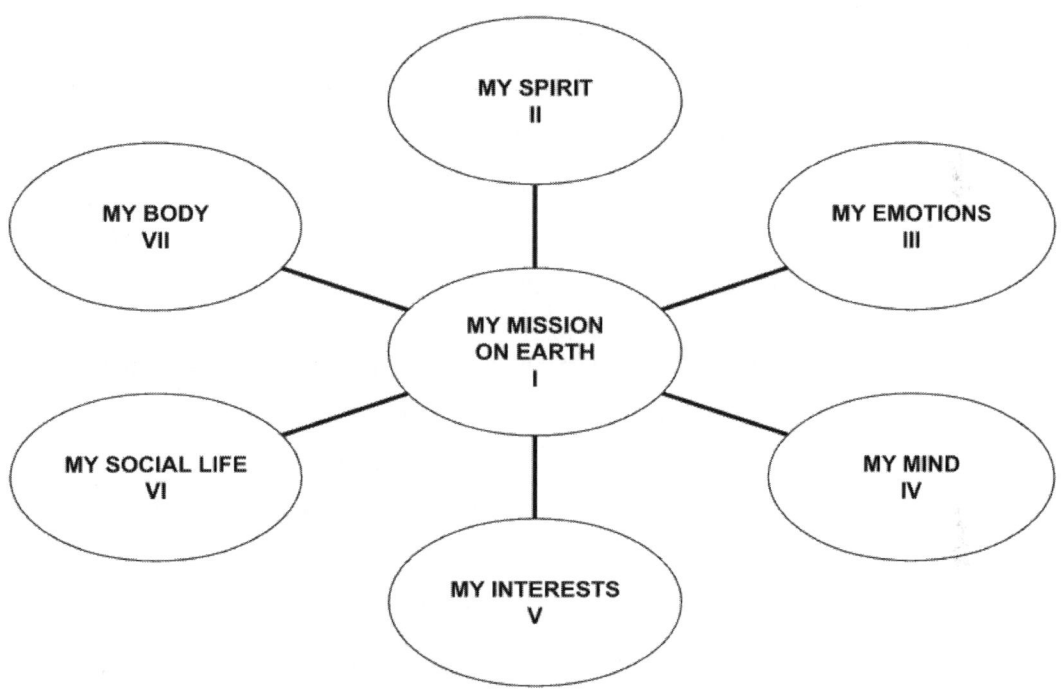

DAVID (CHAMELEON) BOWIE

What about, say, the late David Bowie's mission? Define him? Possible? I mean, given every label is a limitation, how holistic could our definition of this multi-talented legend be? When alive, feeling himself not of the earth, he was always trying to decode the entire puzzle of authentic 'ME-ness'.

Ask how might this star have defined himself more fully? By his next acting role, poem, painting, composition or song lyric? He was known to cut out English phrases, mix them up then, selected by him in a supposedly random order, link them together into a lyric. That was allowing what he called 'unconscious intelligence' to operate until, that is it made 'just enough sense.' Or was that more like a monkey throwing a bucket of paint at a canvass and the zoo keeper selling it as significant art? I do not jest or sneer. Practitioners of the I-ching would approve of trusting such guidance.

In later years, after having assumed so many different personas and tasting so many varied experiences without 'English' inhibitions, Bowie often ended up saying, 'That's NOT where it's AT', Without debilitating disillusion, still in all ways moving forward, he wrote more and more for himself, not for his besotted fans. An Old Soul is more rich in colourful fragments than any ancient mosaic before being assembled into a museum's recognisable picture.

Did this multi-instrumentalist pursue his varied 'incarnations' with such determination because of his divine drive to complete his composite Self? By continuously reinventing his androgynous nature in action, he stayed single-minded and true to his range of inborn inclinations and skills. Spotted at primary school as 'vividly artistic' with a poise 'astonishing in a child', Bowie nonetheless failed his Eleven Plus exam. Like fellow traveller Liz Dumbell (no pun intended!). In fact, Bowie stated that he learnt more by expressing himself than through anything ever taught him by schoolteachers. Maybe, as with us all, the word 'self' should often appear as 'Selves'.

Refusing to become a tradesman, David Robert Jones changed his name as if that was also part of his contract with the Divine, even if it meant exploring drug addiction. What seemed to be consistent was Bowie's restless search, on behalf of us all maybe, to become an icon for the age; a symbol of these uncertain times of transition.

Ironically he did not enjoy performing since its took him away from his real work, defining himself ever more fully. Through his real work. With more Self-worth, is not life more worth living? Reportedly in awe of the universe, by 2005, Bowie disregarded religion having eventually become dissatisfied with much of the Buddhist teaching that individuals do not possess eternal Souls. Not that 'Soul' is a term they use. Anyway, after studying with Tibetan Lama Chime Rinpoche. Bowie said, "Questioning my spiritual life has always been germane to what I was writing. Always." One of the world's many Holy Books offers this quote: 'God will not change the people until they change what is in themselves.'

JADED JAKE

But what about our young head-banger, Jake? Does he not also have a birth plan? So conditioned had he become by state schooling that he had allowed himself to believe it is the job of adults, not he himself, to 'get ME!' What if teachers, instead of trying to turn the lad into a social serf, a wage-slave, the school had treated him as a unique human with hidden gifts? These interests, when identified, could become a central passion and driver making Jake's life meaningful to HIM and socially, more useful and productive? All Souls are surely equal in potential but NOT in experience. Because of freewill, it is our Self-chosen experiences – both inner and outer - that make or break us. That said, we at ATMA are pioneering person-centred approaches to love and learning. Such programmes as MY MASTER LEARNING we see as complementary to traditional politically imposed lessons in the 22,000 schools in the state sector.

How are the finest foundations of learning 'who we are and why' really best served? By studying logic, grammar and the dates of dead monarchs or presidents? No wonder those with even a touch of the Indigo Consciousness fall away from mainstream education. Even so, as I write, there is a surge in the number of 'Free' Schools available. Controversially, they have the same status as academies.

Could that be because of central 'censorship' before state permission is awarded a so-called FREE SCHOOL status? However, enough options are still not offered by our legislators. Yet optimism, like infinity, prevails. Not having to follow the national curriculum, Free Schools have more flexibility over staffing. That gives more control to heads, teachers and governors but not, crucially, to the children themselves; in the main the main, that is.

Will future bewildered students like Jake be also banging their heads against the walls of Free Schools?

To politicians and to bureaucrats, let's make this plea: kindly see shortages in teacher recruitment as with doctors, a symptom of the same malaise. Too much state-imposed tedium and stress through inhuman workloads; paper records deployed as a plethora of superficial tick-box exercises.

How much more goodwill might be salvaged if teachers were give more time to listen with modest respect to complaints from the field? Yes, it is easy to point fingers at non-specialists, educational or medical, but a child's first group of teachers is the family - and whoever complained about non-specialist parents not being trained? Let's instead see supply teachers as the equivalent of Victorian nannies. Such surrogate parents specialised in character building. They chastised the young in their care with slogans like, "Can't? Child, there is no such thing as CAN'T!"

Time now to consider a character-building programme more suitable to the requirements of today's fast rising consciousness.

Lacking in Self-awareness, let alone Self-worth, at his level of spiritual development, Jake would be unable to rate himself above the gutter. And currently, our society is littered with those disabled by the rigours of an over-'mental' educational regime unsuited to their unrecognised emotional needs. As with disabled veterans from the fields of battle, often with similar mental troubles, time to recognize the need for more resources dedicated to rehabilitation?

'Sport has given meaning to my life, a structure,' says one war veteran.

We at ATMA would like to see us develop into the Educational Invictus for those suffering post-traumatic stress disorder (PTSD) from the 'blackboard jungle'. These battle-scarred survivors of all ages need to find better ways to 'give meaning' to their blighted lives.

Records show that, of all jailed prisoners, 42% have been excluded from school. A damning indictment of the current education system fast becoming a global blight.

Increasingly, a growing number of casualties of imposed academia get trapped in mental institutions; or prison. The indifferent law of Cause and effect is reflected in the indifference of state legislators. For us tax payers heavy costs are involved. To stay out of jail, a young recalcitrant social rebel on his last Court warning, costs the British taxpayer about £4,000 a week. Multiply that by hundreds and shudder.

Not so, prison tutor Elva Longfoot, Her "Temple of Learning" has an unorthodox approach to education which greatly reflects our attitudes at ATMA. To quote Peter Stanford, Observer, 22.05.16, "...She offered short courses that taught the inmates *to know themselves* as a way of preparing them to learn English and Maths. That was *the right way round*, experience had taught Longfoot, if they were to be persuaded that education was the *key to unlocking their own potential"* (our emphasis).

THE CIRCLES OF LIFE

As a postscript to the above, it is worth mentioning that in Finland, as if honouring our god-given freewill, early schooling is not compulsory. So no spoon-feeding from the age of three. The teachers' working attitude is not so much 'you get taught by WE grown-ups'. But more,You yourself learn in your own playful way - as you more or less wish'.

The results, unlike in the UK, is the reward of all but full school attendance throughout. These children remain more engaged, I submit, because the early lessons link with the creative principles of the universe. This is perhaps easier if you see these as the gift of love and trust given to each experienced and therefore not innocent child as Soul. Each accepts the invitation to explore its existence through making free choices and learning from their consequences.

Then thank Funland (oopse, Finland!) Let's now rejoice that these Finnish children experience many lessons out of doors in nature and address the Circle of Life. This surely is a more beneficial educational foundation than learning to read too early, not people, but paper. Spirituality, what is not grounded is no earthly use.

Our team working with ATMA further suggest that the Indigo students of all ages have a pressing need to continue linking the 'natural' with the SUPERnatural. What's more, we maintain that since so many of them claim to remember previous lives on earth, the Circle of Life should be enlarged to include past lives, theirs specifically, if only explored as an educational supposition,

Not, of course, as an imposition!.

Such insights can be engendered by asking one and all, 'Who do you think you WERE?'. As for yourself, please note how your answers to this query relate to WHO YOU NOW ARE - because of all the earlier choices that formed your present spiritual status?' So WHO and WHAT were you? How empty life can seem to the super-curious is if these nagging questions remain unaddressed.

Is all this absurd and insubstantial speculation, anyway?

Even if this method is deemed to be mere indulgence as in fairy stories, find children of all ages, like my late mother and one girlfriend, who can remember aged six, actually seeing a fairy.

'ONE sighting only?' you might well ask by way of

seeming not at all suspicious*!*

Myself, knowing the fairy kingdom to be true, there was no need for a viewing of these magical elementals.

The true Indigo consciousness does not need such proof, anyway.

I know fairies exist, together with a Pan-ruled kingdom of many assorted supernatural beings.

By the same token I have never seen - only sensed - the presence of a ghost. If in doubt about the ethereal masons of matter, consult the Findhorn Foundation, the magic garden in Scotland.

And, if so intrigued, the book below...

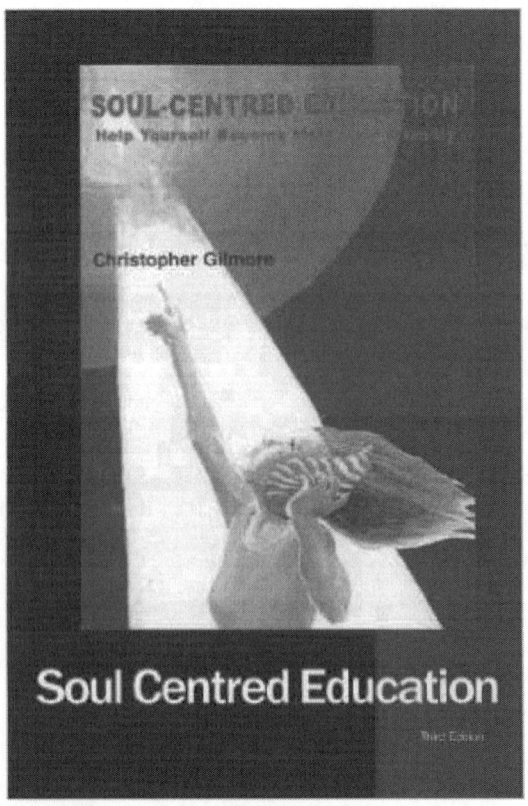

IMPOSED EXAMINATIONS?

In England as I write, there are three competing examination boards, at least one of which has been in the press because of 'administrative' mistakes. This rivalry to recruit ambitious teachers and their scholars can tempt any one of these companies to lower standards in order to raise their company's profits. At that the lowest level, fear of poverty is what helps society's power-freaks to keep us in a state of stress and servitude. But that is our personal choice, like all responses to life's challenges. Fortunately for evolution, most scientists and artists are innovators, if not mavericks.

Educationally, this probability is the exact opposite of what commercially-minded governments want. One theory of privatising companies is so that more of them can thrive financially! - and whatever the cost to the complaining customer who these days is likely to be judged to be in the wrong. As for poor service, how dare they object? Hasn't the taxpayer spend a fortune on educating them to be humble and compliant? Decades ago, rebelling schoolchildren in France were complaining, 'They never *listen* to us!.

Although I failed maths and science at school, I can still see that my weight would be the same no matter from whom I bought my bathroom scales. However, if I belonged to competing 'weighty ones' in a slimming club; one that set the same targets to be reached by every slimmer on the same day of the year, I can well see the temptation to fudge the results. Not me when I mention that, though a failing schoolboy, the adult me was praised by an Ofsted inspector as 'a sometimes inspiring teacher.' Yet cheating in examinations has always been there and overlooked by folks who are more inclined to sustain an educational image of good practice, than to reveal damaging truths.

Alternatively, did I fail maths or did the schools I attended fail me? Meet Roy. This drunk I met in a bar. He also had failed maths at school. Did that make Roy, like me, an Indigo? My question, your answer! Hear us out, please. Roy, at the age of 13 (unlucky for some), got thirteen sums right. His teacher told him so.

But no marks.

When Roy asked Miss why he had been failed, the teacher said because like all students (as if already cloned in her mind) needed to be able to say how they had arrived by the right route to all the correct answers. Roy was rendered speechless. Although he just 'knew' the right answers, he could not explain his reckoning. Instead, his 'reckoning' became like self-punishment. For years hooked on alcohol he was amazed when I declared, "But Roy, you're psychic. Congratulations - have a fruit juice. On me!"

An illiterate friend of mine who left school when he was 14 could strip down car engines and reassemble them without a tutor or guidebooks. If young today, he'd be failed by teachers because he could not write down how he could it.

Benjamin Stubs was praised after a brief Ofsted inspection. "Nice to see laughter in a maths class," was one of the private comments made. My friend supports the individual free will of each college student to grow self-responsibility.

How?

By acknowledging their attitudes to the work in hand. Boundaries and appropriate behaviours are more easily established then, than through hectoring or relying on IMPOSED regimes like the present blanket Academization of all schools. By involving his classes in many human ways, Ben engages their Self respect and from that, gains their loyalty. So no shouting, no threats.

Yet one of his students the Ofsted inspector observed was using the 'F' word. Ben's response was playfully to wag his finger, saying, "The only 'F'-word we want to hear in a maths class is 'F for fractions!'" Laughter, goodwill and the best in human relationships preserved. And Benjamin so far is an unqualified teacher, one who defends his approach against would-be detractors - because as seen now by Ofsted, it works!

Yet where is the archive of such items of good humane practice? Do 'they' favour public blame and shame rather than detailed praise that might improve the engagement of others in education?

Benjamin was not mentioned by name in the printed report from Ofsted or the praised strategies offered to others as a template. My own guess is that all lesson plans that include more artistic than scientific ingredients, in the ways delivered, connect more holistically with students likely to be more receptive than being passively subjugated to lectures.

Back to Benjamin Stubbs. I quote him now from a post on Facebook: 'Working in a college I hear many students debate what they should do and what courses they should study. I also hear many parents talk about the same too and many times anything in the 'arts' gets pushed to one side for it having no 'substance'. Teaching Maths you would think I would be 'Team Academic' but I'm not and it's frustrating to see this 'slight' ridicule and disregard of the Arts even from our Government etc.

'The truth is we all love the Arts, in many different forms and we owe a lot of our great memories of Performers, Musicians, Dancers, Singers, Writers, Directors, Artists, Comedians etc. Yes we need Maths, English and Science based subjects but also need the ARTS.'

For millions like me who found mathematics a headache, another friend, the teacher Erdal Kamal, has devised a game like 'Snap'. This playful approach to learning the times tables up to 12 times 12 is called POWER TABLES, a game I recommend for struggling students of all ages.

Brought up in a materialistic, mechanistic and mechanical school systems, the sixth sense and the fourth dimension are mostly ignored despite this being the age of quantum physics. Yes, left over from certain religions, the dangers of unreliable psychic energies are well documented. Rightly so. But with this proviso. Just as energy can neither be created nor destroyed so, as Indigos can often intuit, Soul cannot be lost, only mislaid. And if Soul is truly indestructible - is in fact an indivisible unit of infinity - we 're-born ones' are being given plenty of chances to 'save' ourselves in our own Self-chosen time. No hurry, no urgency - unless like many Indigos, you want to mop up all your karmic lessons and at last, graduate from the bottom classroom, Earth. This wish if most fervently wished for by the world-weary amongst us.

As one unique Soul we're entrusted with our multiple personas, gifts and journeys. Aura readings, astrology, numerology, palmistry, muscle-testing, these can all be part of our magical aides helping us to find our true selves before accepting the limiting assessments of others who would control us. We all have our share of electromagnetic energy, so we all share the same dualistic propensities to enable eventual promotion into a harmonic unity with Divine Spirit.

Think of Spirit as electricity. It can kill us or illuminate us. What a blessing that after the blackout we call death, it turns out to be an invisible swing door. That being so, how about an holistic health check?

Inside all pains resides a gift

Off Soul's Mission we cause a rift

Our Birth Chart records

With Truth what accords

Lessons learnt allows Soul's uplift!

In the next chapter, more 'romantic' musings for you to you with, if you so choose·

7 DALAI LAMA'S TESTS

Without the skills as state required

By parents kids then not admired

To prevent home rifts

Kids suppress their gifts

Breakdown later and early retired?

We all can benefit from expressing more fully our complete potential. Therefore, our ATMA Playshops are all tailored to fit the unique requirements of each individual who chooses with us to further explore and polish up their treasures within. How? By regaining Self-WORTH through SELF-evaluation. For that to be most effective, we claim, you as your best Self should lead the way.

A true leader never looks behind to see if s/he's being followed; while a true teacher aims to 'lead out' - as in 'educate', the authentic purpose of schooling as an ideal. The teachers often most cherished and remembered are those who somehow lighten the load for all concerned, even if it means subverting the strictures of their training. Hence, we might say, that schools, unlike FACTories, are more healthy when nearer to the educative delights of the arts as in 'showbiz', rather than keeping a narrow focus on 'profits' as in Big Business.

Our varied team of freethinking Enablers recognise and encourage your innate abilities. By helping each to identify, incrementally, what you most need, the dull gemstones that lie dimly dozing in your heart get polished till you again shine with the sunny optimism of a child.

As a reminder, the Latin derivation of our word 'education' is 'I lead forth, I take out. I raise up from out of myself.' This best done without a drug-induced 'high'. In this age of iClouds, iPlayers, iTunes, iPods, iPads and iCals, how appropriate is that! Yet educationally, how long till the little 'i' gains a capital letter signifying the potential autonomy of each Life-Long Learner?

How many children of iParents - single parents seeking individuality and maybe being accused of selfishness - have children who seek more autonomy and will eventually join the growing number of 'singletons' when adult? Maybe, like their parent, these children may hold onto options for which they seek no authentication, despite educated mentors who insist on 'evidence' to refute their opinions.

Such kids may well be Indigos·

In schools many might have felt trapped, what with teachers insisting on expensive uniforms (£10 an item) only to exclude pupils who express themselves, or imitate peers, by appearing with an 'extreme' haircut, ear-studs or coloured streaks in their trendy hairstyle.

As if by excluding such pilgrims experimenting with their image won't breed rebels, and maybe angry criminals or, worse, angry knife-brandishing ;warriors'. Again, as if we can rear innovators, scientific, artistic or social reformers, by standardising children. The future of society rests surely, more on the individual than on ageing institutions, what with a uniformity across the board often supported by parents in case their offspring lose out in life?

TEACHING AS ABUSE?

From Churchill and Einstein to a one-handed concert pianist, somebody might count up how many successful individuals refused to believe the over structured teacher who rated them as 'hopeless'. Cannot selective disobedience be the basis for individual wisdom - and in all ages?

In independent schools in which none of the youngsters need free meals and share spiritual exercises with the staff, many become successful. It can be said that the privileged who pass the 'poshness test' are most likely to reach their life's goal. Contrast the numbers of scholars who qualify for the top universities and, through these, often acquire the top paying jobs, so certain are they of their right to succeed without burn-out. Hence, in the UK in 2015, 43% went to Oxford and 32% to Cambridge, whereas only 23% went to Manchester. Yet the posh boarding school I went to closed, well before at present numbers of private schools, as write, can hardly afford to stay open.

I myself have no Degree so am more fascinated by those school drop-outs who eschewed academia and, as an Indigo or not, followed their central gift and Self-chosen interest into acts of social usefulness. All forms of passion, like an overflow of energy, need to share. However, specialisation is not easily accommodated in 'Comprehensive' Schools; even though they boast of 'a broad and balanced curriculum'. Exam subject choices are given to teenagers, but if such choices do not fit the providers' prevailing remit, the system will impose choices on students.

Immediately it signals to the overruled scholar that their inconvenient main choice/talent/aptitude is not only unnecessary but also, for the most part, that their plaintive appeals remain non-negotiable. What an all-round waste of potential. No wonder the word 'vocation' is now so out of fashion. Switching on the radio then, the news of a 16-year-old boy hit the airwaves. He had just been knifed to death by a fellow schoolboy. That news broke many hearts as I strove to see the page as I finished this very paragraph.

The massacre at America's Columbine High School in 1999 seems to have spawned too many copycat shootings. The inner 'life calling', a phrase used by the mother of Dylan, one of the premeditated teenage killers, ignored in a homogenised and secular system, is killing to the creative human spirit. Hence, murders on the Campus?

October 2015, also in America, that was a year in which 294 mass shootings occurred and, in one U.S. School, the 45th incident was recorded. And still Western politicians colonising Third World countries with their system of schooling fail to ask what it wrong with it. That same week the press showed a photograph of an American security officer. Tipping a female student onto the floor from her chair, he then threw her across the classroom floor. The girl had been asked three times to leave the room. Eventually, the exasperated guard was filmed, saying, 'Either you're coming with me or I'm making you!' What a state school motto that might make.

Let us try to understand this girl's resistance. No evidence is offered here, just an attempt at long distance empathy by asking these questions. 1. Did the girl want to finish a project, uninterrupted? 2. Was she afraid of another bully, waiting in the corridor to duff her up? 3. She felt so inflicted and insulted by the tone of the guard's voice, she refused to comply? Had she been so diminished by didactic teachers always being told to stay quiet that she felt her own voice and opinions were worthless? 4. Was she already afraid of her over-authoritarian dad as a representation of adult maleness? 5. Was she a victim of sexual abuse?

Please now consider for yourself what aspects of her intransigent attitude was being here demonstrated. Not got the time, OK. Who said that? Oh, a nerve-shredded and over-stretched teacher. Sorry. One acting as a loco-parents of the said student. It might be that her parents also are too overworked in providing the wherewithal for family survival to sit down and listen to their hurting daughter. Sorry.

ROMANTICS' MUSES

Back in this country, more abusive adults. I gleaned these examples in an article by Mark Wakefield. 'Are schoolgirls fair game for teachers?' asked the headline. What is questioned here is how many fragile and needy teenage girls form crushes on their teachers.

In this article boys were not included; yet having taught in one music academy, I saw that cross-generational 'crushes' cannot be limited to any one gender or age group. And music especially can stir romantic longings, especially in one-to-one tutorials with musical instruments exploring mutual harmonies. Given 'stalking' can also be non-ageist, the adult professional is obliged to protect their charges like a deputy parent despite the temptations of mutual attraction.

Deja vu? What an Indigo teacher might sense - again with no direct evidence - is that the child and adult romantically attracted might already have been loving partners in a past life. No excuse that if so. Rightly, many will agree.

Remember though, the press persecution footballer Glen Hoddle received when suggesting those with physical disabilities 'deserved' their condition? It still seems as difficult for believers in reincarnation to come out of the closet as for those in public sports to admit they are gay or transgender. Children struggling with such issues should be encouraged by more worthy adult models who have achieved peace of mind as well as a successful life-style.

KIDS COMPANY

Still in the UK, Kids Company, a defunct charity that gave shelter and support to the footloose young nomads walking hectic streets, often homeless, the empty husks of youngsters feeling discarded by

155

all in their painful world. That sanctuary for them, founded by Camilla Batmanghelidjh, was closed down by politicians whose job, arguably, like that of Camilla's devoted staff, was to save youngsters from, at worst, suicide. The predictable(?) result was a wave of angry stabbing, four suicide attempts and one murdered youth called Jerrell.

Before that, according to his grieving mother Amanda Elie, Kid's Company had played a major role in his life. What does the government want now? More street riots? In Croydon, burnt-out shells of houses and shops made rich pickings for looters and such devastation provided good business for property developers. Another example surely of private pennies prioritized over suitable support for the poor struggling plebs; legions of young criminalised victims of society's democratic decisions. Cash can be counted but how do we count the cost of human unkindness? While society at large is mesmerised by money, this so easily measured when lacking, we still have no measurement for compassion.

Danel M Haybron, sociologist, has produced a checklist of ingredients that constitute human happiness. How daring! He supplies the letters S.O.A.R as an acronym. We suggest you search your inner Self first, rather than be told what the academic has decided the four letters stand for. On reflection, he wondered if he should have added contact with the 'natural world.' Good. Very worthy. Yet might we of ATMA whisper yet another addition would improve contentment? How about contact with the SUPER--natural world as indicated in the seminal book SUPERNATURE by the late biologist, Lyall Watson? Those who reject religious teachings might ask themselves whether or not that stops them being spiritual beings.

Think of the inter-denominational mountainside country, Bhutan. Freedom of belief is allowed though the state religion is Vajrayana Buddhism. That country's GDP is measured by human happiness! Commons' sense? Horse sense? Well, the week the United Arab Emirates announced they were to appoint a Minister of Happiness, scientists discovered that sensitive horses respond to happy faces as well as calming down hyperactive learners of all ages.. Too many sad years since I read a book entitled HAPPY CLASSROOMS. (University of the Trees Press 1982.)

In the UK currently, universities are vying with each other, luring potential students into their courses with free football tickets and iPads. And that despite the estimated numbers of graduates presently working. That number is said to be 1 in 10 employed - in the low wage economy. So much for the mental achievements of education's elitists with their emphasis on producing material benefits across the board as well as to business boardrooms.

COSMIC CLASSROOMS

But life should not be boring. For, as in all ages past, Earth is our chosen classroom. It has all ways offered a vast range of alternatives; be they our attitudes and/or our actions. These choices suit this binary universe. For every upbeat motion, there's always a downside; this emphasised in the taking in too much alcohol or illegal drugs. (More on ecstasy and MDMA later.)

I was about to write about the learning opportunities afforded by modern hi-tech iTech consuls and the like, when an item on the daily news challenged my present viewpoint. How exciting!

It seems that University researchers on over 800 schoolchildren, showed that the longer a sedentary child stays glued to screens (mobiles, PCs, iPads, TVs etc), the lower their eventual grades when sitting school examinations; another sedentary hazard!

My own caveat would be this: academics measuring children's performances on tests prepared by other academics, all students meant to excel in the same systematic academic way, this is enough to make any Indigo sympathise with unhappy peers who too often take to knives or guns in order to kill the pain of imposed learning styles, systems that can kill individuality and its unacknowledged hidden gifts. For all of these avoidable distresses, our ATMA team offer complementary strategies. We hope these will be tickling enough chakras for you all to keep on turning over yet another new page!

Personally, would you enjoy questions like, 'What here and now would you most like to offer yourself by way of making improvements to your life?' This remedial approach could reverse much of life's-long learners' restrictive conditioning. Maybe the 'How?' is more problematical than the 'Why?'

Starting from childhood, those physically taller than us as kids, habitually decided what was good for us. What's worse, without asking questions that might, educationally, have expanded general goodwill by our opinions being taken seriously; and/or, negotiated. by way of encouraging expansion of every subject on offer

If for example, we thought it fun to burn down the house. Like one of my brothers. One way of inconveniencing the family, this being so much more possible in these times of latchkey kids. Yes, and their pressured parents with two part-time jobs and all life's necessities too darned time-consuming despite zero hour contracts. No time left for cooking a family meal, or having an open forum discussion with the whole family under the same roof. Remember dining-rooms? Families are mixed ability learning groups, so expected is a variety of fads, phases and picky eaters.

Oh, the damage lack of money imposes. It restricts the poor in too many ways, picky eating being an unaffordable luxury. But money is an energy and like all other currencies can respond to our belief system - even before Bingo! Luck is more than a lottery. Like love. The curious are welcome to listen to ATMA's MP3 *Money as a Mantra.*

Finding life's obligations overwhelming, parents under pressure with children under pressure, with teachers under pressure led by politicians under pressure, no wonder the exponential growth of RECOVERY COLLEGES and other remedial outfits like HOME-START for volunteers to visit stressed-out adults. All of these activities are mostly to protect the struggling injured of a sick society, from life-styles that are a burden on the taxpayer.

'Remedial?' we ask - is that word is still politically current? In every way, what an expensive waste of resources, both personal and social. But maybe that suits our rulers. Given how much employment if dedicated to those psychologically crippled by systems to which the victims cannot relate, the Remedial Business is so thriving that the employment figures must have politicians singing from the same balance sheet. The fact that we taxpayers might be better off if society was not breeding so many victims seems not to appeal to those who want power and ownership over our diminishing resources. And such disabilities more often than not get exacerbated in uncongenial classrooms.

In 2015, examination boards, accused of yet more careless (unfair) marking systems, 77.000 papers had to be reassessed as original grades got challenged. Each re-marked paper was at the cost up to the sum of £60. A charge too expensive for the families of our poorest attending food banks.

Another example of the rich State, by promoting Academias, Colleges and Universities as being the surest way to achieve a successful life, operating a form of hidden psychological blackmail aided by Ofqual. True, there is a refund if the examination grades are regraded. Yet as I was finishing edits on this book, it was announced that Ofqual, the Office of Qualifications and Examinations Regulation, was seeking to stop private schools from sending in scripts for reassessment of awarded grades. Maybe, despite the above, the societal tide is changing towards more of a people-friendly modus operandi. Perhaps this is indicated in the next section. Let's hope so.

NESTA

Improvements to be long-term need to be preventative, not just remedial. And that fact, as in patients aiming to save the National Health Service, is currently being addressed by NESTA, the innovative charity that helps people and organisations to bring great ideas to life. Yours? Mine? OURS? Indeed, the NHS of Liverpool has inaugurated plans to give more emphasis to preventative modes of addressing transitional ailments.

No. We at ATMA apparently did not fit their remit. If you agree with the following please ask why the originators of the NESTA philosophy could not see the merits in what we offer. Namely this basic truism: only conscientious pro-active Self-awareness can prevent certain aspects of personal pain. The central examination in all lives is in all ways, always SELF-examination. As one Chinese student at Cambridge expressed it as..a place 'To explore inner talents'.

Whether born a pirate, prelate, politician or pauper, no Soul is innocent in heaven. Only when they reach Earth they are unlikely yo recall their lesson plan - unless of, or near, the Indigo consciousness - to which they agreed pre-birth to follow in their present life. Believe this or not, throughout all lives YOU are the chief subject, not an object. Any more than every student of every subject anywhere, or at any time, is ever truly objective. Today on the news it was stated that even scientists now acknowledge that the Stock Exchange is run more on emotion than on so-called mathematical logic.

For NESTA 'innovation' is the buzzword. As they tackle the need for a sea-change in the National Health Service, we see as an even more radical need; the dire need for a sea-change in the provision and delivery of education. To link these two needs surely, is to accept the NESTA emphasis on 'person centred' approaches to individual responsibility.' The evolution of human consciousness requires it. Attention! ATMA Enterprises, this is your life's vocation.

Soon you will be introduced to our seemingly frivolous counterpoint between the words 'vocation' and 'vacation'. Well, in the NESTA publication The Future of PEOPLE POWERED HEALTH, another pair of mirror images appear on the final page. It is headed, FUTUREFEST. One paragraph each introduces four areas of future developments. They are Love, Play, Work and Future Thrive. Which two do you think have exactly the same 69 words? A repeated hint: The evolution of human consciousness requires it. Again, attention!

ATMA Enterprises, this is still your life's vocation, despite all early rejections. In fact, our intentions found some support from the Minister of State for Children and Families at the Department for Education, At least our poster inviting recruits was placed for a week in the window of his constituency window. Thank you Edward Timpson, MP.

MINING ME - c/o ATMA

Time now to become more of your own true person, inwardly and outwardly, both enjoyed as play and as work. Unless, like us, you see them as being complementary approaches to all of life's offerings. On the ATMA website, you may already have seen MINING ME. In this Self-searching survey you were invited to rediscover your treasure-chest of gifts, the gems hidden within Soul, heart and mind.

Now, if you feel like a true Indigo, you will wish to explore these treasures. Not to change your own beliefs or lifestyle without your say-so, of course. No. So why bother searching more deeply inside yourself, unless to change? No growth without change, no matter how challenging. What's more, belief in the unselfish Self rather than in the State and its bureaucracy, is the trump card we all have hidden in our pack.

Or will we stay like the old lady who unconsciously admitted, 'Doctor, doctor, I does enjoy bad 'ealth'. Or to her vicar, complaining,

'Yer Reverend, such a sufferin' soul the likes of me is sore tempted to pinch yer poor box'. No point in saying to that poor old biddy, 'My dear child of God, you are a victim of your own consciousness. In any case dear, let us be clear. You do not have a soul...' 'Look 'ere Mr Vicar, I'm not bleedin' barefoot. Not yet...' 'God be praised, such a humble pilgrim. But consider this. We sinners do not have a Soul. we ARE Soul. 'These boots see, they got one each.' 'God is so generous, lady. Be grateful.'

A poor personality can despair. But no Soul can ever be lost. Like optimism it belongs to indestructible infinity. We all are given gifts beyond and before words; but not before the formative agencies of Sound (wisdom) and Light (knowledge). This open-hearted invitation from 'Upstairs' makes us all our own central and sacred Sentinel. On our very own invisible staircase.

As witness to this truth, in one of my classes a little seven-year-old mystic asked us all, 'How do you know you're not the centre of the universe?' Such a wise Indigo. Jon was back on earth as a spiritual teacher and he knew it.

Despite our individual approaches to learning ever more about 'me', our ATMA team is united in our belief that each person has a specific purpose for being on earth now. To live on purpose, inside out, is our highest achievement. By that means we can complete our lesson plan with Spirit by facing all of our selves and by balancing out all levels of love. To grow in Self-esteem from the very centre of our unique being, to earn that in full, what an opportunity, what a privilege!

Who would not wish to become a fluent writer in action of their own life story; to become more useful and beautiful, not just in one's own eyes, but in the eyes of Angels and Earthlings alike?

For this to become increasingly true, let us help you to find your own way. Love is never too late. So whether an ageless adult or an ageless child, there are techniques to aid Self-recovery. But better still, as already mentioned, ATMA offers a rich range of ways to prevent much stress and tension, starting, ideally, with the very young at heart of any and indeed of every, age. Rejoice!

OUR INNER SATNAV?

In wishing to remind myself how the present Dalai Lama was elected, I consulted the Oracle, Google. In the search bar I used the word 'test'. Lo and behold, there and then I was lured into a personality test. Would it be anything like our MINING ME?

On life's journey, can we use intuition's inner voice like our own private Satnav? As did the present Dalai Lama. He is the fourteenth in line of that teaching order, one of seven children. And Christians please note, he was born in a stable. Indigo students, being as much lateral as literal in their thinking, might well enjoy numerology and astrology by way of a balancing factor to so-called logical mathematics. Me, too. So being fourteenth in line, that makes him a

'5' in numerology whereas in astrology, he's a royal, home loving Cancer - though by way of sacrifice and personal safety, he no longer lives in Tibet.. As for the number five, it represents occult gifts; think of the 5-pointed star as shown in these pages and elsewhere. Maybe inwardly as well...?.

The number seven being so significant to us at ATMA, you'd think I was keen to plunge into the personality test posted on the Dalai Lama website. But observations based on numerology made me wary to proceed. Yet despite reservations, I did so. And my suspicions were well-founded. See if you agree with my conclusions.

After several warnings about cheating (charming!) they present a range of choices. For example, What qualities do I associate with 5 (yes, five) assorted animals. These ranged from a tiger, my favourite, to pig (which I don't eat). Another list of 5 questions involved colours. It asks participants to associate yellow, orange, red, white and green with their loved ones. For at least two of these colours I chose members of the ATMA team. Let them guess who and why! Throughout the quiz, so-called right answers were provided.

Surprisingly, I found in matching the colours with my five chosen friends mainly turned out to be very relevant. Coincidence? No. That is the cop-out word sceptics use when challenged by phenomena they do not wish to associate with divine guidance, the results of all-inclusive consciousness in harmony with our inner nature.

Interesting? Not my favourite word when used as a lazy blanket cop-out. As, for example, when readers call my writings 'interesting', I know they don't 'get me'. I've learnt not to sulk!. But back to my main point - what this quiz offered as the correct answers. In telling me that a tiger stands for pride and that coffee stands for sex, I nearly felt insulted. And that despite the compilers' claim there are no right or wrong answers! I now dismiss the whole exercise as twaddle. Do ask...so what...?

MINING MY MIND

Just like school tests, the uncertainty principle is avoided in order to control the populace with an examination system that, in *order* to pass *muster* - note these two military words - scholars have to submit their free will and its free spirit to a system that to the Indigo sensibility, is anathema. Thanks to ATMA visitor, Bow Focske, we gratefully accepted her offer to turn our own person-centred quiz MINING ME into a two pronged probe. We agreed to the need to balance our heart-based version with a second part underscored by a more academically rigorous remit. To make it more head-centred, a complementary second version seemed to be an all-round advantage. And that despite a long experienced practitioner working in the field of the mentally challenged, praised our original survey.

Lindsey wrote:

MINING ME 23/May 2015

'I wish that many of the other 'mainstream' psychological well-being research questions were this insightful and illuminating! How much better the outcomes would be! Instead of huge amounts of money being spent, on CBT (Cognitive Behavioural Therapy) through the current so-called IAPT (Improved Access to Psychological Therapies) - to make minor steps forward, the money could be invested into an approach that could really provide some actual relief! As discussed at the Crewe event today, I would love to do what I can to help! With love, light and laughter, Lindsey xx

Thank you, Lindsay. That was from a professional in the field. Like thousands of others taught how to help society's victims, is she also suffering like others known to me because, according to the 'ethics' of their contract, they are not allowed to mention God or to engage with anything that might be called 'spiritual'. After all, we don't want the injured of academia to go mental. God forbid!'.

Notice how many atheists, confronted with troubles, call out for help, starting with the expletive, 'MY God…'? One living Master of the Ancient Wisdom teaches that there is a spiritual path for every single Soul, including the atheist. No creature is excluded from the love of God, be they a dog, duchess, dustmen or a Don. I'm not convinced any university Don would give much credence to the person-probing quiz on the current Dalai Lama site. But what about our ATMA offerings such as MY MASTER LEARNING MENU?

For the more academically trained mind, heart-centred data can be rated as too flaky to count as acceptable for research findings. In

168

order to get a wider interest in the work of ATMA, Bow wrote these suggestions for our website: www.atmaenterprises.co.uk.

She suggested we invite some parents of Indigo children to write comments on how they feel about forcing their children to go to a school where they know their child's needs are not being fully met. I have a friend who is going through this. Her child is labelled 'naughty' because he knows the system is wrong, for her. Yet she feels powerless to blame the school system. "I mean, as parents in surrendering our power to the school, we never think we can challenge it. So it's teachers and parents against child." She ends by asking that all adults become inspired to put each child first.

Bow explained that as part of her research for her Masters she had read of 3000 studies on spirituality and health, physical and mental. Every one of them uses a different definition. Bow then said, '...we can build a school...with teachers who possess emotional intelligence, empathy and morality.' She is developing a framework using secular language to explain spirituality in order to increase equanimity, increased self-awareness and pro-social, equality, all of this aiming towards the kind of universal morality expounded by Lawrence Kohlberg. Change attitudes, systems and outcomes change'.

People who are spiritual (even if they can't define in word) lead better lives. Maybe this should not be stated as fact given how defensive others with very different views can be. But mindfulness in classrooms is gaining ground, mediation being practised and, hopefully, in PSHE classes, children are being consulted more than before. That is, rather than just being instructed about Personal, Social and Health Education..

Indeed, currently the spread of interest in Buddhism has encouraged mindfulness in order to strengthen one's own inner resources. They dismiss the accusation of 'selfishness'. As individualised ego, we folks need to manage their own challenges with enough confidence before aiming to help others to improve their life-style. Then researchers of any age or belief system might well be employed studying how inner work in the human brain produces better chemicals in the body.

Therefore, by making MINING ME 2 more head than heart-centred, ATMA could be said to represent the virtues of both the left (more male Western?) brain and right (more female Eastern?) brain. The two sides of the globe, like the two lobes of the human brain, need to work together in closer harmony. Just like a sound marriage.

"DIFFERENT...BETTER..."

For over 3 hours they were in my house. My guests were two unrelated 9-year-olds who together were being home-educated. With them was their mothers and one suckling a babe in arms.

The five of us played educational games for just over two hours. Taking a non-ageist approach, I offered a series of intriguing experiences to help awaken Self-Awareness in action. Rather than use 'class' time as a form of mind manipulation, the four involved were invited to explore their own choices.

For this, they were given a variety of multi-sensory strategies, personal free will in all ways honoured. While observing the individualized results of such choices, we all could be encouraged to see that every choice has a consequence and that to take ownership throughout, can help build Self-confidence; more so than say, blind obedience to didactic decrees with the promise of Degrees as passports assuring success in your chosen field.

At all ages, the human spirit can be impoverished by too few flights of fancy; feelings blunted by a paucity of enough experiences to stimulate emotional well-being. The human mind can become a prison cell instead of a beehive if locked in with too much so-called logical exposition. Likewise, the human body, as with all of our other faculties, need regular stretching for us to become healthy enough to fulfil our unique potential. Such personalized approaches to love and learning is being pioneered by our ATMA team.

Asked afterwards for feedback, the 9-year-old girl in my house considered her reply before volunteering her opinion; and that without looking at any of the three adults in my front room. Sitting on the only sofa with her friend, the 9-year-old boy, her words were...'Different...better. Like heaven.'

What pupil In any Faith School might make such a comment? Surely, the compliment was offered because that youngster felt her faith in herself being re-enforced. Our innovate team is always happy to network with like-spirited educators of all ages. I myself run talks and 'PLAYSHOPS' on the theme of INDIGO EDUCATION FOR SPIRITED LEARNERS. To learn about our corporate offerings, please turn to the last chapter. There you will find a succinct list of all of our present offerings. There also, you surely will find something to inspire, motivate and incentivise every one of you - in your own chosen ways.

Now a member of the local CVS, in their Autumn gathering, before our own inaugural public meeting in December, Hilary Newhall was asked to lead a session on Creative Approaches to Volunteering. As a team we relish producing Playshop presentations on any unexpected topics to fit outside requests.

When in Comprehensive Schools I used to encourage Creativity Across the Curriculum; hence my series of ten DOVETALES like MIGHTY MATHAMATICS – More Fun, Less Fear?

DALAI LAMA'S TESTS

Back to the saintly man himself. The current holder of the role of the fourteenth Chosen One was selected in ways that the Indigo could find fascinating and valid. This is what I wish to further unpack now.

Talk of superstition, coincidences and fairy stories, accusations marshalled by agnostics wary of working with Spirit consciously as with mystics; or unconsciously, as with all of us day-and-night dreamers. Yet legend had claimed that the head of the deceased thirteenth Dalai Lama had miraculously turned. Instead of staying still in his grave and facing South-East, the head had turned to face North-East, towards Mongolia.

There they found a 2-year-old boy. He was presented with maybe five pairs of objects. Would the little lad choose the items that had belonged to the previous holder of the role, or not? The suspense was short-lived. In each choice made, the child exclaimed, "it's MINE!" In every case he was right. The objects had been used by the previous Dalai Lama.

At best, the true Indigo feels blessed. But also sometimes has personal quibbles with the Creative Spirit. Yet whoever stays in contact with their beloved, both using cell phones, during their earthly communication, decides NOT to BELIEVE in mobiles? They KNOW both receivers work to mutual advantage.

Yet let's accept that there are legions of sceptics. To the multitudes of our fellow human beings feeling disconnected from mythical consciousness, what dare we suggest? How angry might they get? Especially if gently we suggest that it is this very spirited and intimate connection with the Creative Spirit that they secretly crave. At least their favourite swear word 'superstition', starts with the prefix SUPER!

Let's now see education at all levels as a means of freeing the personal spirit. We therefore warmly hope that those of you who

173

took part - or are about to participate, in our MINING ME 1 and 2 Survey, use these first healing steps to a manifesto for the making of a better ME.

Such person-centred strategies we are continuing to develop since ATMA Enterprises emphatically does not subscribe to a consumerist one-system fits all - or else FAILURE.

No learning program will completely nourish unique YOU: not unless we honour your free will as so with each and every student. To quote Plato again:

'Imposed education will never remain in the Soul'.

As with the test on the Dalai Lama site, why TELL me a tiger represents PRIDE? What if I agreed with William Blake and saw my tyger as representing 'fearful symmetry'. That painter and poet as a school phobic let's add to my list of historic and pioneering Indigos. Just as I'm grateful to welcome the Dalai Lama's recognition, as a tiny boy, of his destiny through what we might call the little lad's gift of psychometry.

As with author Moyra Caldecott. She gave me permission to dramatise her novel *King of Shadows*, this well received by an audience of schoolchildren, although their Headteacher admitted to me that he did not understand the piece.

However, it was an act of psychometry that inspired Moyra's trilogy, *The Tall Stones*. In placing her brow on standing stones in a

Scottish Stone Circle she had been shown a re-run of the historic battles fought around that area. Yes, the Gifts of Spirit are timeless. And for us all, one lifetime or another. And in every one, in love with all of life, there is all ways another lesson. Having the longing to learn them all, how liberating is that!

ROLE-PLAY AS RE-PLAY

As a young professional actor I was always puzzled by my own inbuilt talent. I knew it didn't 'belong' to me. It felt more like I'd somehow borrowed it. How did I know without instruction how to wield a sword, proffer a snuffbox to my nose or, when playing in Restoration comedies, place a beauty spot on my face? Enough circumstantial 'evidence' for me to accept reincarnation as a reality?

Exploring mementoes left over from my childhood I found a painting I did at Primary school after seeing my first pantomime. Also in that album was a picture of me as an eight-year-old, playing Humpty Dumpty in a version of ALICE THROUGH THE LOOKING GLASS by Lewis Carroll. Under the photograph, some adult had written 'Actors to be or not to be'.

Three points on that if I might stay personal for a bit longer. It was in acting so many roles all round Britain as a versatile actor that I realised I was re-enacting many roles I had played throughout the centuries on the stage called Earth. This realisation in fictional form is explored in my novel ALICE IN WELFARELAND.

I do very little acting these days but I have produced a number of YouTubes under the umbrella title, REJUICED SHAKESPEARE. In one, I appear as an elderly Hamlet. Well, two Hamlets. In the second one, I act out the famous 'suicide' speech again. In similar rhymes and rhythms of the original, I explore death through the eyes of reincarnation.

Cheeky, eh?

But fun!

Still speaking from the Indigo part of my nature, I see the real subject in every lesson presented by life, as MINE. Is that any more vain than those taking regular Selfies and posting them on social media? Your decision! That said, my third childhood reference is here on offer as personal evidence of my 'Early Inklings' and their prophetic insights.

Academically I was deemed a dunce. That's what late developers were called back then. I'd been relegated to a Crammers to brush up my mathematics.

The professor failed!

The fact that I preferred to brush up my Shakespeare was not considered important. Even though, by then, I was already in love with the works of Wordsworth Blake and the Bard.

No apologies now for another biographic fact. In my unhappy teens I was writing sonnets influenced by these writers. Many of the following rhyming lines, I now realise, illustrated the aching Soul seeking its true Self. This spotty-faced youth felt marooned on Planet X yet scrutinised himself as if a deserted alien with no nearby oasis.

Below then is sonnet number 5.

Like all the other 4, their overall title was:-

SONNETS TO MYSELF

The sombre searchings of a secret soul

Oft are prompted by a turbulent trust.

Some doubt man's mission as a spectral goal

And he who lives will diagnose his dust.

In those mellow hours of melancholy

When unintelligible tear rides white cheek

Some say, 'Be blithe for brooding is folly';

'A fool always fails when he's forced,' you speak.

But the salt of that tear may well create

For weeping is expression, this a birth;

And each mental birth must have pain for mate,

Fruitful labour begets you then sweet mirth.

When despondent with yourself and your doom

Thank God for the gifts that express your gloom.

I promise you, this has not been polished up to show how clever that pimply teenager was. However, now I'm a few years off departing into my well-diagnosed dust, I've just counted up six aspects in that sonnet that were prophetic.

Like compass needles, they all pointed to my future. Indeed, in reading this, you are also part of my present life-style.

So again ,welcome!

So we see that this past lad, in writing in the third person, prepared him for the detachment an actor must adopt, especially when in his sensitive teens playing a murderer like Othello. The instructive experiences of this role are recorded in my award-winning essay for United Press, 2010. Called BEHIND THE CURTAIN, it describes my advancements in understanding though being a character actor.

Given our present passion in reforming the delivery of personal education, all of those subconscious early insights were predictors. Agree? Is it therefore not too absurd to state that the insights in that sonnet indicated my hidden embryonic interests? Yes, my main passions were then invisible; like buried daffodil bulbs before they become golden trumpeters greeting each new springtime.

Well, here I am working with ATMA, our team all sharing a passionate concern for the welfare of insightful New Age children. Do they not also nurse within their secret selves a simmering idea of what their future holds in store? That being possible, educationally, made manifest, how productive that realisation might become!

8 EARLY INKLINGS' EMPORIUM?

Picture a house in your Soul's eye

Draw it on paper, sun in the sky·

Add one pond, one tree,

One path, snake and see

Yourself more clearly from on high

'Give me a child until he is seven and I will give you the man.' This boastful quote is from the teachings of Francis Xavier, one of the founders of the Society of Jesus. I wonder how much his namesake, the present Pope Francis, would want the teachings of that Spanish Saint reformed.

I was brought up in a Jesuit boarding-School, not from seven but from the age of eleven. Told I was a Roman Catholic, I suppose as an 'ex' now, I'm classed as a heretic bound for purgatory or worse. But surprisingly, the priests' timetable allowed room for free artistic expression. Thursday afternoon, in the school's theatre hall, a whole year group expressed many aspects of creativity as we boys explored our interests and talents. I swear that in those presentations we teens learnt more about our true Selves and hidden needs than in all the mandatory Catechism classes. But what if such open-hearted opportunities for Self-discovery had been offered us at 4-years-old?

First, let's explore this propensity as illustrated in the lives of others. Hopefully, this could sometime in the future also include your good self - or selves'!? (To thine own selves be true'?) So now you might care to test yourself as to your own inner signposts. For me they started when I was about three. Or earlier.

Sue Klebold is the author of *A Mother's Reckoning* - a parents' guide. The proceeds are going to mental health care. She is the mother of Dylan, a teen who wanted to destroy Columbine High School and all within it. As a newborn in her arms, she had a premonition. She says it was as if a bird of prey cast a deep shadow over her child, one that boded some unknown future disaster. This insight she forgot until after the massacre in Colorado.

But, behind the veil, the signposts were there.

How about your very earliest memories? What if they had been similar to mine? Want to test your powers of empathy and insight? If so, here we go...

The beat of a big bass drum was the core of my first vivid memory. As it grew nearer and louder. I howled with tears. Watching the military band marching past the house, my nose pressed to a windowpane, tears were streaming down my cheeks.

Why? What had been triggered?

It took me decades of wondering. But significantly, I never forgot the experience. Again, why? I now think the impressions lingered by way of reminding me what are my bespoke lessons this lifetime. And the message of that hidden mission? Must it remain wrapped up in attitudes and actions I'll never comprehend, or master? Again, were there lessons left over from earlier lives on earth?

Eureka*!* Of Course, YES*!*

That is, unless through proactive awareness, I address all of my issues that reek of unfinished business, spiritually speaking. Would the seeker in me succeed in unpacking all inside, like those intrigued Ethiopian children the cardboard boxes that seemingly had just dropped from the sky?

Well, while the military band stirred memories of me marching towards my last death as in World War One, myself a paid killer.

My other indelible memory related not to a past lifetime but to this present one. It was a hunt for Easter eggs. They had been hidden all over the drawing-room. How I relished the search. How I was certain I'd find what I was looking for - Cream chockies! That approach, dear readers, justified the accuracy of my own early inklings and illustrated my character so very soon after my latest birth. Since then I've never stopped searching how to lay all my 'eggs' to rest, not not just gobbling down Easter Eggs.

But first, I had to find them. After lots of brooding, I believe I did so. Well, after a triple heart bypass I'm still alive so guess there's still one or two lessons still hiding from me. Or am I hiding from them? Anyway, it seems to me we all are born with a clutch of realisations that we are invited to hatch out ourselves through bespoke experiences.

Another seminal discovery is that as soon as Soul shows a willingness to learn all the lessons on this lifetime's lesson plan, the divine guidance greets our efforts and aids the process with showers of blessings. These confirm we truly are on a path of ascendancy. Hear, if uou wish, my MP3 entitled SEEDPODS and ASCENDANCY, a collections of poems.

Like you also. To celebrate that certainty (not a popular quality these days), you can prevent further uncertainties by asking 'Upstairs' to send direct evidence you are on the right path. But if doubts seem to be entrenched, there are techniques to remove psychological blocks. If you so choose, we can show you how. Hence we invite you to explore more deeply your own Birth Chart within the context of universal principles.

ATMA Enterprises offer an idea for a series of TV programmes. The working title is EARLY INKLINGS' EMPORIUM (code named EIID). Interested...?

ABSTRACT

Everyone being gifted can become an expert in some area of life. Many restless and dissatisfied children, with whom teachers struggle, might well have been as quick as the present Dalai Lama, when a 'fearless child of only two, he identified what matches his life's future map and journey. This is said to be tree of all Dalai Lamas past and yet to come. By doing so, they could now be happily developing their Self-chosen skill with passion, making it the core of their personal curriculum. Certain personal traits can be detected in my DVD, EARLY LEANERS KNOW LOTS. At such a tender age they indicated their present character and at best, stay true to their mission on earth.

WORKING ETHOS AND ATTITUDES

Having enjoyed for ten years sharing thinking skills with 4-year-olds, I can vouch for how much inner knowing even toddlers can demonstrate. For this to operate to optimum levels of mutual learning, a rich environment needs to be on offer. Too many teaching regimes look for what their students CAN'T do.

Two points on this.

In such systems, the agenda and timetable is already set. Set and settled by those who for their convenience need to secure accountable systems of control in order to acquire degrees of conformity.

With passive compliance, how debilitating is that to the diversity innate in spirited learners of all ages?

Let us instead concentrate on what each of us as adults, with little ones in our care, This CAN do, perhaps better than their peers?. Education offered as a shared adventure, as in Forest Schools at which ATMA member Cynthia Moore has enabled woodland crafts and survival techniques. In National Parks, personal gains on offer are multiple; plus the possibility of not just learning practical skills but sharing together inner and outer travel. As in the best of storytelling. In a forest sitting around a bonfire all enjoying magical tales, the whole spirit of the group wafted away into regions way beyond logic and pain. Youngsters stimulated into thinking for themselves, can ponder on deep riddles than defy prevailing rationales; like, What the is best shape to describe imagination? Not for them the perceived need to parrot phrases to please and placate the adults from whom they seek attention and approval. Or not.

Like four-year-old Sonia less than a week in her first primary class. When asked by her mother how had she enjoyed the classes, she just sighed out the single word: 'SLOW'. Mother advised, 'Be kind to the teacher. She's doing her best and with so many in the class, she has to think of everyone'.

Did such a heartfelt plea work? Not a bit of it. Two days later, at the end of the three more lessons, Sonia went up to the teacher and said, "I'm bored, Miss. Can we move on, please?' Sonia already sensed what she needs to be learning, but never having been consulted, intuitively, she felt insulted. She spoke out for a growing number of silenced little learners.

CHILDREN'S NEEDS REVEALED?

Imagination when enlarged, offers more choices than imposed lessons. The key question is when and how can the making of choices be best implemented? Do adults organising regimented regimes with firm controls offer enough choices? Or co-operation? No. Hence the blanket impoverishment of Self-esteem (?).

Yet do we not all learn best by making choices and, by these, learn that each choice has consequences? State-imposed constraints inhibit such luxuries. Too many voices needing to be heard; too little time before the next academic test. All these constraints lead to downsizing individuality. Free expression not encouraged across the board might suit the future job market; albeit that each citizen may have to tackle five totally different jobs in their working life. That is as well as facing enforced retirement due to robots rendering workers, especially blue-collar workers, redundant.

In preparation, this is where children's playtimes can be so crucial. And, importantly for this TV submission, diagnostic. Watch the children define their interests and budding aptitudes when their choices are triggered by impulsive curiosity. In such sessions, modes of Self mastery can be tested; safe experiments conducted, all such young impulses led, it seems, by an innate 'knowing' - and best seen BEFORE being tutored by adults. It might be in making paper aeroplanes that can fly - first steps to becoming an expert in aerodynamics?

Or maybe, helping to feed an injured baby hedgehog - the first indication of a budding vet? One little girl took three packets of biscuits and, placing them in a line, shunted them along making the sound of a steam train. As if such a young child was determined to stay under its own steam and drive forward her own interests. But STEAM! How did the child know such locomotives ever existed?

Moving further back in time, consider T. Rex. This unique relic of a once common dinosaur bigger than a rogue elephant is called Sue. It was identified by palaeontologist Peter Larson. Since the age of four he dreamed of finding a tyrannosaurus. I'm sure you're noticing how this apprehension of the little boy's future career beautifully serves one of this book's major themes.

At every age the need for personal power can be channelled into mastering Self-chosen skills. As one irritated 7-year-old said to us in one philosophy class, 'Why explore other planets when we haven't got this planet perfect?'

Seeing sage nods from most of his peers and a look of approval on my face, young Martin got me thinking.

If every child can see the world as her or his oyster, then education should help each one to find their own unique and precious pearl. For this to succeed more holistically, the culture of education needs to become artistic, even in the sciences. An eleven-year-old reader of my DOVETALES INTGRATED SCIENCE - Love Before Learning? considered his response. Lighting up, he said,

"Fancy, poetry in a science book!"

Fancy can inspire maybe even more than a daily dose of facts.

BY HOW MUCH CAN YOUNG CHILDREN INDICATE THEIR FUTURE?

FIRSTLY, but in tandem with other researches, a widespread survey with adults can yield valuable insights. As with 'Robert; a father of four boys. As a 3-year-old, he 'knew' he was in the 'wrong' body. How much stress might he have been saved if, like the three-year-old boys who 'knew' they should be girls in 2016, were fortunately supported in their gender changeover?

Thus they became members of the increasing number of people who as children changed sex. As with other cases of transgender and the legalisation of same-sex marriages, might not these developments indicate a transition in societal consciousness; a reassignment of incremental options?

Records could be collected as to the earliest memories of selected subjects. Collated, such notes will show in how many ways these earliest memories could be seen as having 'predicted' that adult's future. We further suggest that the crossroads faced by most individuals appear around every twelve years. This checked out might reveal, for example, a serious mid-life crisis with that person say around the age of 48.

Maybe that was a signal to get back on track and to rediscover the earliest inklings of the way their life might best have developed if such whispers had been seen as at a higher level of practical wisdom than the unhealthy path instead chosen.

SECONDLY, the parents who have accepted the value in this EIID approach to Self discovery, might give permission for their children to record their earliest memories.

The children could be watched to see in how many ways in voluntary play, or perhaps in non-directed chats, they seem to 'predict' their future. Yes we know not all children will become pop stars or train drivers, but nonetheless, their filmed ideas could be revisited every twelve years and reassessed by them as to the accuracy and usefulness of their own earliest INKLINGS.

THIRDLY - and most challengingly - in this area of personal 'knowingness' we offer the biggest idea yet. We identify this by the letters EIEID. Namely, EARLY INKLINGS' EMPORIUM

Aptitude tests can be found online. Some are for measuring verbal and numerical reasoning. Handy for applicants for university and for assessing the capacities of potential employees. As for leisure, adults might have visited the National Gallery, viewing paintings there while specially composed music played in the background.

At Tate Modern the Sensorium offered a range of artistic experiences devised by perfumiers and chocolatiers, touch specialists and sound architects, all giving members of the public multi-sensual adventures, all thanks to an outfit called 'Creative Studios'. Admission was free but those under 18 were not allowed entry unless signed in by a parent or guardian.

Why?

Why should adults have all the fun of exploring their senses? Not to exclude traditional play areas providing sandpits and water, our vision for expansion is not just epic but seminal. And as such, frankly, expensive to mount.

But the international consortiums could be persuaded to take part; regardless of whether or not such donations had the contractual obligation to carry forms of advertising. The list of possibilities is enormous. Below, a few are suggested by way of making a start.

Big business might donate hands-on items and/or funds to support the ideals here visualised as a way of helping to ensure a more useful and contented citizenry of the future: an unstable future like as not, one that will need more inner resources. Flexibility goes with creativity. And the future might mean for each person years and years of enforced leisure, and that imposed in the middle years despite the state's retirement ages being shifted upwards. All such possible contingencies should be considered.

A good preparation for such a possibility is flexischooling. This is successfully operated by headteacher Janette Moundford-Lees with Lynda O'Sullivan at Hollinsclough Primary Academy – http://hollinsclough.staffs.sch.uk/Flexi.htm. These ladies I met on a day conference on Alternative Educational Futures hosted by Peter Humphries, chair, trustee and a director of the Centre for Personalised Education – Personalised Education Now (CPE-PEN).

The list that follows is indicative rather than definitive. The inspired ideas of organisers in the field will always trump theoretical notions dreamed up in an author's bedroom. However, picture EARLY INKLINGS' EMPORIUM being housed in and around somewhere like the Alexandra Palace. Ambitious? Innovative? Maybe so, maybe not.

Remember the bored little schoolgirl Sonia? Now meet Sandra, her mother, Born an orphan she was markedly abused in the children's home; so many scars that if she had a daughter, never ever would she allow her anywhere near situations that might injure her to the same degree as 'bastards' were treated years back. That is why Sandra removed Sonia, her wise daughter, labelled with 'learning difficulties' from her primary school.

As part of her home education, Sonia took her 4-year-daughter to Ikea. The idea was for Sonia to choose items for her bedroom. Everything from the colour of the walls to the shape and size of her wardrobe. The tour of that family-centred Swedish emporium did not start on the top floor. There a range of complete bedrooms, including nurseries, was on display, each in a different design. No, Instead, the little girl was invited to roam the huge building and its rich displays of diversified goods and, in choosing their route, relate with her what engaged her imagination from moment to moment. The girl's learning curve in selecting from such a rich mixture of colours as to her choice of carpets, curtains and other fabrics, a privileged responsibility so very stimulating and informative. Likewise, in her other choices as in the shape and size of furniture. It provided lessons not just in design and styles, but in spacial mathematics, as in the working out of what fixtures and fittings matched the little girl's need to factor in functionality in all of her domestic items being installed.

How she grew to love her bedroom. Absorbed by direct experiences so early on gave her a sense of responsible ownership. So much so, there would be no need as a teen for her mum to be crying out once a week, 'Sandra, I'm sick and tired of your untidy bedroom.' No wonder as a 4-year-old she had found pre-packaged top-down

195

school lessons a bore. In contrast we suggest, to the ATMA vision of an Early Inklings' Emporium.

This is by way of suggesting a list of firms and other institutions that might contribute to EIEID. Given the above real life anecdote, top of the list now must be is...YES, you've guessed it...Ikea! Now to add to our wish-list:

Alternative technology

Lego-land

Disneyland

London and/or Whipsnade Zoo Pets' Corner

Alton Towers

Interactive Science Museums

Educational publishers

Argos.

Film companies

Apple technologies

B&Q

National Theatre - dressing up possibilities.

Science labs

Farmer's Weekly

Orchestras

Art Colleges - paints, crayons etc

Electronic portrait galleries

Costumes of all ages/ cultures

Car manufacturers

Gym toys with sports' gear

Kitchen fitters

Multi-faith artefacts

Football Clubs

Modelling Agency with cosmetics

Travel videos

Planetarium

Dance facilities

Miniature villages etc

Clay plasticine

Hospital equipment and Health Services

Arboretum and Garden Centres

Times Educational Supplement - TES

Google/Microsoft

Hamleys

Mothercare

Early Learning Centre

National Parks

Sailing Clubs

Seafaring adventures

Aircraft and UFOs

Transport museums

Farms/Zoos and Animal Sanctuaries

(Whose first word was not mum, but zoo?

Think of a famous naturalist.)

Baby prophet of what he'd to do

Gerald Durrell's first word was ZOO!

Recall your first deeds

Soul's calling shows leads

Were such predictions true for you?

EMPORIUMS' OPERATIONS

Now for its practical applications. No matter the scale in size provided or the range of human interests and occupations covered at ground level, as a play area, every one should be chosen to intrigue and engage little children's innate curiosity. Ideally, every response should be theirs. Maybe with a suitable adult to hand, if that is what any little boy or girl requests. The whole of the educational areas of activities could be fitted out with CCTV cameras allowing for playback recordings. Children, with all-round permission, could be watched by experts in various professional fields of human behaviour and development. Yet the revolutionary notion offered here needs all involved to agree on the possibility that even a 4-year-old as potentially in charge of shaping his or her own choices regarding their individual 'destiny'. That is whether any one child of either gender plays with a doll or a toy car. And if empty cardboard boxes are made available, watch in how many ways they can be transformed by the imagination of happy children.

SIGNIFICANT GLIMPSES?

All of this emphasises the main point we would like to keep repeating. In potential, each child can be allowed to become her or his own expert. That is the educational advantage of letting children LEAD their own learning patterns rather than being cowed into meek obedience which can too early close down their ability to think things out for themselves, thereby depriving them of making their own choices, including attitudes to all experiences, whether rated as pleasant or not.

Another point; in being presented with filmed evidence, those watching the screen, including the filmed child, will see for how long each child was activity engaged, or not. As with body language, observers can see the character and nature of the filmed subject being illustrated in action. For further clarity, maybe ask these questions:

1. Given a vast range of choices, what prompts the child's curiosity?

2. Do your choices indicate pending aspects of character?

3. Was there ever a look of immediate interest; perhaps even of some mysterious form of familiarity?

4. Did she or he need instructions?

5. Or reject them when offered?

6. Again, was there any area of interest to which the child kept revisiting?

In all of these aspects being demonstrated pre-school, is the child's specialist area of potential expertise being revealed? If so, in a complementary way, could not that central revelation become the centre of its own bespoke curriculum?

Why? Because as each learner experiences joy in making a relationship with some skill base, as with being in charge of a puppy or a radio-controlled dog. Such experiences could, and indeed arguably SHOULD, be the foundation of the child's Self esteem. As I have written so often - A Happy Childhood Lasts a Lifetime (if not, why not?).

For instance, if a TV company got behind this innovative research project, a documentary on EARLY INKLINGS might film all of these developments, incrementally. To monitor the surveys' progress, the willing children and adults could be filmed thenceforward every twelve years.

TV PRECEDENTS

The precedent has already been seen to work. Previous worthy TV programmes on suchlike themes were a success. Witness, Granada Television's UP Series and dating back to 1964. SEVEN UP. Both generally asked, 'What becomes of the dreams of children?' Nothing worse for the future of our society than adults underestimating our children's potential.

As for the Stanford University 'Marshmallow Test', that also showed early choices indicated the future propensity of each baby participant. Researchers followed up the toddlers' responses. Which of them unattended would be tempted to gobble down - or not - the sweetie left in front of them?

Remember, the babes were asked to trust the tester's promise that TWO marshmallows would be theirs if they left the first one untouched long enough. That done, a double was on offer, two sweeties a reward worth waiting for. Or was it? Result, the babies who resisted temptation and relied on their own Self-discipline (and put faith in the presenter's promise) became more successful in later life; a phenomena not unknown amongst those who left school ages 16. Like me!

'The Secret Life of my Family' was another TV programme to consider. From the Victorian habit of rich folks touring the slums with their guidebook, up to the descendants of such paupers, the researchers showed pattens of human behaviour that stayed mostly similar down the generations. The cycle of deprivation, however, could be broken. The major key in such transformations was the environment of the children being studied. That of course, could not happen without engaging each child's bespoke gifts and willing 'permission'.

While a scientist's X-ray microscope can peer into an acorn, no oak tree will be seen there. Any more than a Pet Scan can perceive in advance the fully matured foetus. But universally, as personal consciousness rises, more perceptive youngsters, attuned to their own spiritual needs, will insist on staying true to their life's mission.

Rebellion will ring a bell with more and more seeking autonomy. We wonder if you agree with our ATMA Team on the ideas outlined above. As you saw fully fleshed out in the section on EARLY INKLINGS' EMPORIUM, we maintain that a personalised inner curriculum resides in the Soul of each learner.

And those blessed with an Indigo consciousness are already sufficiently awakened to the invitations that are implicit in their Self-awareness kit. Through a variety of worldly and other-worldly experiences, a drive that invites total energy-management, all personalised skills honed and monitored through the Higher Self.

Not possible? Or is this age of the Selfie indicative of too much self-obsession verging on selfishness? In evolutionary terms, good questions demand ever better answers - YOURS!

Let them be beautiful useful and life-enhancing. Life needs vision, passion and guidance.

Working towards such a worthwhile prospect, in the next chapter we introduce you to our pioneering Team of Enablers. Please welcome them.

For we humans become the Hope

All round help will help each cope

Inwardly Self-made

With some outer aid

Let all folks become their own pope

9 MEET Y/OUR ENABLERS?

CREATOR more than a notion
See dewdrops fall in the ocean
They are one another
We our own brother
ALL'S Evolution in motion

73 - That was the number of listed words I selected to count up in the Collins dictionary lent to me. I reached number 43 before all of these words starting with the single syllable SELF adjusted itself to the slur word so popular with those who wish to make us feel guilty. That barbed word is 'selfish'.

But Self development is not necessarily selfish. This all depends upon the motive. Certainly it is not selfish when you stop feeling bad when others make you feel guilty for causing their hurt. Wake up, victims. Fell less guilty. Take responsibility for 'allowing' your pain to penetrate; even at worst, to define you.

Think of flexible Yogis blissed out, not stressed out, contemplating in the full lotus position as, deeply, they breathe in and out with a mantra on their lips. Yet life can feel lonely, especially as erstwhile friends slip away thinking you weird.

But self-fulfilment needs sustained self-discipline. As persevering readers will appreciate by now, again it is the highest possible Self we speak of here.

As our holy gardener we can learn how to treat all pain as manure; compost that will help mature all our buds until we beam out our beauty in full bloom.

You who feel clearer about your spiritual past will also know your present status is recorded - and not just on Facebook. If you already keep a clear idea of life after your next death, you may not need this next section. I myself when reading books often skip passages. Just like perceptive students cherry-pick extracts from set books; the extracts quoted to please the tutor's prejudices. I use my inner Geiger-counter to guide me to the parts I myself then subsequently need.

Selfish? Self-seeking? Or just down right self-reliant? So skip away, dear Indigos, while others are invited to remain. I mean, who can define your needs better than your Highest Self? Not your mother, brother, sister or God parent. What follows now is the chance to taste the following warm-up. We might call it an OMlette. Why? Because each of us as Soul will become truly omniscient, omnipresent and omnipotent. That's it, folks - so a bright future awaits us all, whatever, whenever...!

If not Soul, who do you think you are? On TV, celebrities are reassessing themselves, helped by researchers into historical archives. Not only murderers have a yen to return to the scene of their 'crimes', so do oldies like me. I have a longing to return to my magical childhood haunts in Cumberland and again link up in the land of the Lakeland poets. And why not? Are we not drinking the same water as the dinosaurs? As suggested in Saint Matthew's gospel, rain falls equally on the just and unjust alike. But the human heart, like a parasol in sunshine, operates best when it is wide open.

While spending most of my younger years seeking the meaning and purpose of existence, I came across books by Doctor Arthur Guirdham. In West Cumbria - as it's now called - he was born. In Workington, the town in which this little Christopher, still wearing cap and short pants, saw his first stage show. Watching that pantomime, quicker than a twinkling, in more than an inkling, in a flash I KNEW I'd become an actor.

Guirdham, son of a steelworker of Huguenot descent, gained a scholarship to Oxford University. In his medical writing he was soon offering an alternative view to mental health, illness and personality. views often in opposition to the prevailing psychiatric movement. Instead, and increasingly, his interest in esoteric history led him into the paranormal and, significantly for the Indigo consciousness, he pioneered spiritual reasons for illnesses, both physical and mental.

For me personally, his later books helped me to become more confident and comfortable with the implications of reincarnation. The book title that resonated with me most was WE ARE ONE

ANOTHER. It includes a sketch by a 7-year-old girl offering proof, albeit only on paper, of memories of an earlier life on earth living with Guirdham and many of his friends.

As with the Dalai Lama, Guirdham describes how just for himself he verified his own insights into rebirth. To further authenticate his research he consulted a Professor Nelti. Often present with them was a Mrs Smith. She related word for word songs that had remained hidden in archives in 1944; songs that were not discovered until in 1967. And that was not all. Astonishingly, Mrs Smith produced correct drawings of old French coins, and jewellery; together with accurate descriptions of rituals, dresses, layouts of buildings and details of family relationships at that time when the Cathars were being persecuted by the Roman Catholic Inquisition whose aim was to suppress heresy.

Historically we, as it were, indeed were often in tribes and thereby in each other's space. A Shaman comes in all shapes and sizes. Same as actors. As for the late Sir Laurence Olivier, watching him in his many roles I thought he was a Shaman. Yes, as Shakespeare knew and illustrated so effectively in his play THE TEMPEST, both the beast Caliban, and spirit of the air Ariel, is in every human Soul. I played both roles. Subsequently, as a quick-change artist, I found I could morph into many a different role, even playing insects as well as well-known iconic figures like the dandy Beau Brummel. As to the former Prime Minister, William Gladstone, the critic of the Daily Telegraph said I looked more like him than did the statue in London's Holborn. Such praise did not change my political views!

This ability to morph into different creatures was a gift of the tribal so-called savages; these transformations helped by dressing up to placate their potential predators. In Elizabethan times, boys played the female characters in Shakespeare; while the tradition of men playing the Dame and lithe ladies slapping their thighs by way of presenting cod male heroes, still appear in Pantomimes. In this context, let's remind ourselves of Metamorphosis by Franz Kafka. In that novel the central character wakes up to find himself turned into a gigantic insect.

Throughout all the kingdoms of creation such as mineral, vegetable, animal and mankind, inwardly in all such manifestations we are somehow one another; all from the same Source; all crafted from the same materials.

Arguably, otherwise, the arts and empathy with even the non-denominational elementals and angels, would not exist. And like singing Angels, disembodied Soul has no gender.

Is not all of Creation made from Sound and Light? Let's put that to the test. Hear the composers of symphonies. Is it not as if their secret Self is instrumental in the search for the Lost Chord, the white noise of infinity?

Watch sculptors, like little gods, shaping clay into human forms, often made in their own image. Or observe frantic abstract painters participating in the rich range of the rainbow's seven colours. As if they also are trying to find a unifying identity in all their restless efforts to reach the Ultimate.

Is that's when my brother learns to become his own complete keeper? Each to their own choices every second...

En route to such levels of completion, combining all roles, watch the writers and actors of 'fiction' express the versatility of the human identity in action. Such a nourishing cornucopia. By experiencing all our universal ingredients in turn, all of us in our own chosen ways are seeking unity with our very essence. Educationally, cutting out the creative arts from learners is to imperil the future of the human spirit. It seeks eternal freedom. Unattainable, of course, without wisdom.

MEET ATMA'S ENABLERS

The longing for reunion

May not be only human

Not lost but mislaid

All God's folks are made

To achieve total communion

The central curriculum for all unique individuals every lifetime is our own consciousness. That benefits from daily attention. When accommodated without the fears that come from being treated as a misfit, all futures can be bravely faced with relish. No matter how or when achieved, Self determination needs Self belief. But just as antibiotics are becoming less and less effective in healing physical ailments, so are the sterile State's remedial strategies that aim to address the injured psyche of its disenfranchised citizens. These patchwork 'remedies' are now also needing more effective strategies.

Time for us to be exactingly true to ourselves. But which set of teachings do we trust enough to believe in? As Bertolt Brecht said in his characterisation of the famous astronomer Galileo: 'Unhappy the land that has a need for heroes.' Film star Sylvester Stallone defined a true hero according to his consciousness. This is someone, he claims, who gets beaten down time and time again and yet eventually stands upright and survives. Maybe it takes more courage for an Indigo to stay true to the requirements of that condition than the bravery required of a gunslinger or a boxer like Stallone. His biography is called Somebody Up There Likes Me. Can any one of us succeed in life unless we each like and believe - nay, know - the making of 'ME' is my total responsibility? What a God-given privilege!

GOOD RIDDANCE, MR CHIPS?

Well, now that teachers, doctors, politicians and preachers are for the most part being less deified by the discerning public, where do we find such healing from stress; except perhaps by turning ourselves into our own hero and saviour? In these 'End Times', many Christians feel an urgency about being saved. But in the age of the Selfie, Savours have lost much of their appeal. Yet a quote from the Talmud reads, 'Whoever rescues a single soul they have saved the whole world'. How do we disentangle these apparent disparities? And can anyone tell me from whence this quote? "The time will come when each will be his own priest". (Answer later!)

Many centuries ago the Hindu scriptures taught about the need for reincarnation. How can that help us? Envisage if you will, God as one big dartboard. Imagine that each newborn cherub is given just one of Cupid's darts. In a Catechism class the child learns that his single dart has only been lent by God. It has to be returned in the same pristine condition as when created. That is, when with free will through a multiplicity of experiences it again reaches perfection. But before death reclaims that single life, the individual on earth has only one throw of that one dart. In short, a one-shot chance to hit the bull's eye. If God is unconditional love, how generous is that?

Yes, the Hindu teachings indicate that our carousels of karma are our own responsibility. Though Spiritual Masters will show the way to the seven heavens, as Soul we are gifted with aeons of opportunities to implement DIY Divinity through countless lifetimes. In a series of different bodies on the wheel of the yearly cycles, we learn through a vast range of bespoke episodes, all sent to test our personal powers and stamina.   Now the Kali Yuga, being the time of karma-come-home, we are in the fourth of these Yugas, the Iron Age. That is our worldwide situation as oceans tides rise, exploding mountains vomit ash and floods and molten fires ruin acres of fertile lands. Historic cities crack open and people's houses fall into craters as, so in wartimes, millions become homeless. Is all this caused by centuries of ignorance of the laws of life and death?

Like Mother Nature won't be tamed, the Indigo children amongst us will only tolerate adult educational 'interference' by either cowering back into their shell and become all but opaque and inaccessible; or alternatively, become so obstreperous as to be as unmanageable and unreliable as the British weather. Especially to the control freaks, will they stay obstinately unresponsive. In short, the assembly-line factory model is now totally out of tune for a growing number of our New Age youngsters seeking their unique way in the world. And that was mostly true when I was in the classroom over twenty years ago. The adults victimised by this archaic system of instruction are today's clients, the therapists kept busy.

We offer our help. So please now get to know more about our ATMA ENABLERS.   That said, I have been noticing that it is almost mandatory for those with even a neo-Indigo consciousness to be somewhat dyslexic! Why? Well, when with SEAL, the disbanded Society of Effective, Affective Learning, they gave me a prize for a competition they had launched. Who would like to write a poem addressing those with dyslexia? ME, please! By way of a prize, they published my winning poem. It was called DSYLEXIC'S DELIGHT. It appeared in the chapter "Creativity the Master Key" in my book "SOUL CENTRED EDUCATION".

YOUTH AMBASSADORS

I write this in the week that the blame for the Hillsborough football stadium tragedy was legally placed at the foot of plodding boots and plotting brains of the South Yorkshire Constabulary. A couple of days after this report, parents threatened to remove their 6 and 7-year-olds on the day they are 'required' to sit new SAT tests. Indeed, by then, over 31,000 parents had signed a petition to boycott such stressful school tests.

We've already seen how a 6-year-old changed the atmosphere in her classroom. Now let me introduce you to Grace, another remarkable school student, and her single mother, Andrea Killeen.

20-year-old Freddie, a natural poet, came to one meeting of our ATMA Team. Albeit he was with his mother, a recalcitrant teacher not uncritical of the current regime. Although having trespecitively haxin g passed his final exams successfully, Freddie agreed to join us an a YOUTH AMBASSASDOR able to go into school assembles and address the students there. Welcome Freddie!

Please now enjoy extracts of a letter sent on behalf of the struggling but conscientious scholar who was suffering from dyslexia, this not diagnosed till Grace was in her teens.

Dear Teacher

I am writing to you to on behalf of my daughter Grace Killeen, as after weeks of thought and discussion between myself, Grace and her teachers we have come to a solid decision in what Grace wants for her future.

As you are probably aware, Grace is the most conscientious, hard working, determined and resilient student, she has held this attitude since the very beginning after working as hard as I'm sure you are aware - to gain her place in your prestigious college, she has never once let this work ethic slip, therefore as she has been putting in 100% effort day in day out from the start, she should be feeling fully confident and prepared for her end of year AS exams in a matter of weeks, however unusually - this is not the case. Since having the dyslexia assessment opportunity we had been longing for, for years (thanks to yourself), and being diagnosed as severely Dyslexic Grace has noticed the significant barriers her dyslexia has withheld for her during this year of AS.

As exams are vastly approaching Grace has expectedly done nothing but keep her head down spending hours of intense study, however not managing any revision! - this is because the time she spends studying is attempting to re-teach her self lessons, sections

216

and topics because as a typical server dyslexic she has found it such a challenge to try and keep up with the teachers speed all year, finding herself missing essential content when it comes to tests - creating unavoidable gaps in her knowledge, we have been aware of this all year but Grace's attitude has been "as I did for GCSE, if I work hard enough I will achieve what I deserve"

However this really isn't the case as it stands, despite her independent efforts Grace isn't achieving to the best of her ability and we believe this is primarily down to the speed in which Grace was expected to digest such advanced information. After Grace finally facing the fact that she can't cope with the way things are - she is working her hardest to digest and understand in time for her AS qualifications but KNOWS only too well that she is NOT prepared for next months exams to dictate her AS grades, the reason why Grace has been incredibly unhappy, unhealthy and feeling so down despite her continuous hard work is because she realizes that her potential is being extremely restricted.

Grace has never wanted to be the most popular girl in the class, she has never wanted to be the most wealthy girl in the class, she has never wanted to be at the top of her class - all she's ever wanted is to be at the top of her potential and achieve/perform to the best of her ability, to be the best version of herself as possible. We believe that Grace's problem here isn't that A levels aren't for her, or that she hasn't worked hard enough, it is that of the speed of which Grace has been expected to endure that has been her flaw, whenever something is re taught to her by her teachers she always claims to gain a much deeper understanding.

Hence, the main request was for Grace to re-do the year's study in order to be on top of the work load. So, thank you, Mrs Killeen, for being such a remarkable mother. Guess why I say that. Well, if you care to re-read this extract, please do so. But this time let me share with you what the whole school faculty might never have sensed. The entire content of the letter, with all of its clear insights, was written by GRACE HERSELF, unaided by her permissive parent.

No wonder, I had already asked Grace to become a Youth Ambassador for ATMA Enterprises.

What an example of the personalized Indigo consciousness staying squarely on the case; the real work being all based on personalized Self Awareness. Self diagnosis, this being the Master Key to one's Self-selected door of earthly success. Staying all the way in charge of life's many choices of attitudes and actions, others like Grace, are bound to earn their best blessings. Grace let's see as a pioneering Wayshower.

ATMA'S TEAM PLAYERS

Please now warmly welcome our ATMA ENABLERS, most of whom like me indeed, are dyslexic. What drew us together is that, despite so many objections and obstructions we all had encountered educationally, most of us have become Self-Made Survivors of the classroom.

If you've already met the core members of the ATMA Team, maybe you're ready to ask 'Well, what else is on offer, guys?' Time to mention that David Renner, a long enthusiast and supporter of these approaches to Self examination, was the first to commit to this cause when we were working under the title INaSENSE. David is a farmer, and '...an abundance engineer, learning to love and loving to learn while continuing to search for the Art of Smart, lazy husbandry.' He is the author of a book about extending the life of a crop dryer by utilising a waste product of sugar beet production.

Sue Bayley I have already quoted. When first reading her 'blurb' on our ATMA website, tears were pricking my eyes. Here is a taster. She states that her Soul purpose was refined at her Ordination as an Interfaith Minister. Faith, like invisible healing, as indeed the help that passes between Sue and those in her presence, is inexpressible. It is these ineffable qualities in all of the ATMA Team that needs to be shared. Sue writes:

"Here I am, wherever I am, shining my light naturally. I vow to see the sacred in my Self and the apparent other, and release them into the truth of who we are."

I would now add:

And to let the world know that each child is valuable… autistic or non-autistic alike. Are we all not 'un-abled' in one way or another, that making us all, thank goodness blessedly different?

Sue is sensitive, empathetic, non-judgemental, a lateral thinker, and someone who can handle the expectations of others with her Emotional Intelligence, Passion and Compassion. This approach permeates all areas of Sue Bayley's life as a qualified Careers Adviser, Body Therapist, Spiritual Counsellor, and a brown belt NIA dance teacher. She is also a Reiki master.

Diane Beechcroft is probably more comfortable with much of the academic word than some of us. Her present list of formal qualification surely emphasise this. As witness this list:

Transactional Analyst Psychotherapist; Provisional Teaching and Supervising Transactional Analyst; MA Counselling Studies; BSc Human Psychology; ACCA foundation in accounts; Assorted A levels and GCEs from the dawn of time.

Diane represents the amazingly innovative of work of Jane Lloyd, and both ladies are available for consultations. Below, please find Diane's personal experiences while working with Jane Lloyd and her pioneering work.

"When I did my psychology degree and trained as a psychotherapist in the 1980s, the idea that what effected your ability to concentrate and learn, or your mood, was considered to be laughable quackery, completely unsuitable for serious study. Yet in 2016 there is scarcely a week goes by without a new piece of research/book/article showing that almost anything can be attributed to how well the microbes in your gut affect every area of your life.

"Jane Lloyd has known about this and been working to balance the gut, now known to be a major area of difficulty, for example, in autism. She has understood that problems in school, and life learning, relate to a complex array of interlocking developmental issues. Over 20 years she has created tests to identify areas of developmental difference; and even more interestingly, has developed ways of delivering balancing programmes to remove the blocks limiting a person from becoming the best version of themselves that they can be.

"Jane uses the word "stress" to describe the situation where a person, or part of the system, is trying to do or complete some action and is unable to do so. Unresolved stress cascades creating an increasingly varied range of problems and often drug-related, symptoms. Because she is an innovator whatever I say about this today will be out of date by tomorrow. The current system involves an unobtrusive radio tag worn so the balancing frequencies can be sent automatically by a computer, enabling the person to come into balance in the most beneficial way.

"An example from me. I have had weight issues since I was 5 and weighed 15 stone at 15. I have never, ever lost weight without extreme dieting, and then the weight would come back plus a couple of stone. When I came onto the programme I was so distressed about my weight and the fact it was going up by 2 stone a year that I was planning suicide.

"The first thing that happened was that I stopped putting weight on. No change in eating or activity, I did nothing different but the weight gain stopped. This was / is amazing. Then I came to understand that I had serious metabolic issues and that it was nothing to do with me, I was not mad, bad, naughty, greedy, lazy….etc etc etc. I relaxed, this helped the programme do its job.

"I have lost nearly 3 stone without dieting, most of it in the last 12 months. That is very good and I am very happy, but it isn't the point. My metabolism is working, therefore my health is improving, my thinking is clear, I am not anxious, I am not depressed, I am learning new skills, loving that process and finding it easier than I did twenty years ago when I was 40. I have not changed, the programme has balanced a range of developmental issues and my metabolism and I am becoming a better version of myself as advertised."

As Diane has said, 'Without passion there is no sense of direction.' And at ATMA her colleagues would add BRAVO, and so say all of us; we all sincerely aim to aid each other and all of our clients, present and yet to come with our unique approaches to well-being. See our list of PLAYSHOPS below. But first, let's introduce some more of the founding team directors for ATMA Enterprises.

Meet David Blackhurst. He designed and built our website as well, I should say, as my own at christophergilmore.co.uk. He thought he might help to change education knowing, even as a struggling schoolboy, that the present system was far from perfect. He has years of valuable experience working with problematical youngsters, these often on the wrong side of the Law. So changing the world through education is now his chief focus. Towards that long range ambition, he is committed to helping ATMA's aims. A visionary some might say, one thing is for certain he has much to offer.

Patricia Mackrell, like others with ATMA, has too many qualifications and experiences of life to list here. As with the others, more of Patricia's details can be checked on our website. In brief, she is a Personal Wellness Coach, and Nutritional Consultant, a NIA Technique Teacher as well as of Infinite Tai Chi. She originally trained and was employed in the performing arts sector and later worked within the media, primarily for Granada Television. A stress-related illness led her into a more natural and Self-empowering life-style, she is studying the healing practices of various holistic therapies, including the Nia Technique (Neuromuscular Integrative Action - see www.nianow.com). Patricia is available for talks, demonstrations, interviews, taster Playshops and can bring an energising and uplifting experience to any event.

Bow Foscke, has already contributed invaluable insights and practical steerage to the ATMA's early stages. Likewise, Roger Peck and Cynthia Moor, Liz Dumbell; but I now happily introduce another highly qualified member of our team.

Meet Hilary Newhall, BA, HONS – DIP LA – ADV DIP – Cert Ed - MA, TESOL   She presents herself as a Learner, Teacher, Landscape Architect, Community Architect and Author. She has worked as a landscape artist and community artist and has also taught English (EFL) in France to children and adults and English (ESOL) as well as garden design to adults.

What with Patricia Mackrell as an expert on wholesome organic food, between all those mentioned here, collectively, we could cook up a bean feast in a Borstal! We have already been designing a series of person-centred Playshops called MY MASTER LEARNING MENU. I hope by now you are able to appreciate more fully our rich range of Enablers.

Every life-long learner has a different metabolism, blood group and preferences of taste. Whether the academic diner is fed hamburger with greasy chips or tofu and millet for most meals, the consequences for the learner are markedly different. The hungry mind also seeks good nourishment. But force feed it with a diet of stale facts and, like obese sedentary geese attached to a feeding tube three times daily, enlarging their livers grotesquely, the intensive factory farming as in the production of paté de foie gras, is producing deformed products. Stuffing systematic mental health-inducing fodder into our young folks without their happy compliance is often injurious. Is it a surprise that that later leads to so many forms of self-harm?

Currently, these drilled children, learning by rote despite Wikipedia, Google and their mobiles, are cowed into conformity. Their playgrounds and sports fields increasingly are shrinking like their initiative. What with sports and arts activities curtailed and discursive discussions limited by tightening timetables, so many rewarding aspects of schooling are now threatening 'the happiest days of your life'.

INDIGO VEGETARIANS

Helped by teachers on healthy eating like our own Patricia, slowly, Meatless Mondays are catching on. This might at last start to reduce the methane gas released from both ends of every 'sacred' cow. And save the planet from the waste it produces which is as much as fifty humans. How do I know this?

The editor of the vegetarian magazine Ahimsa, Nitin Mehta, gave me a free copy. He is one of the group of Asians who set up a new Free School in Croydon. He has said that he would be interested for we at ATMA to stay in touch with developments. As with most aware parents, when a child enables itself it is already on the way to independence, an essential ingredient of autonomy. It may well start in the high-chair, the toddler refusing to eat beef, drink cow's milk or chew peanuts. That is, even if earlier discovered shoving a handful of soil into a willing mouth. Well, do not the aware ones reborn 'remember' that all minerals come from the earth?

The central article in Ahimsa (Summer 2014) was devoted to "FARMAGEDDON: The True Cost of Cheap Meat" a new book by Philip Lymbery and Isabel Okeshott exposing the real cost of meat consumption. The obesity related health costs to the UK tax payer is £1.25 million annually. And in a year, 25,000 patients die of drug resistant microorganisms. The book also records statistics relating to the worldwide destruction of habitats for bees; the unhealthy effects of fish farming and the water tables being poisoned by overflowing effluent from pig farms distorting the eco-system.

More information can be found on www.ciwf.org.uk, the site for Compassion in World Farming. What with worldwide, 4 billion suffering from malnutrition. It seems to us, that no modern learning system should ignore world facts that can damage everyone's future. That we can see people growing sick, that is no reason for students to nurture their own patch, the health of our shared global village being fundamental to earthly survival. Fortunately, many New Age children are passionate about ecology. A global challenge.

Shall we decorate such gloomy data with tinsel as we annually drape dying Christmas trees? Can we not see recycled glitter in litter? Sustaining meals in trash bins parked at the back of supermarkets? Death is not a disease but life can become so by going too far against the laws of nature. And as for the fundamental needs of human nature, can they not be better met? Here now are just a few more thoughts on this dilemma; themes that interest many of our future citizens but not yet tackled often enough by well-heeled adults. Our ATMA Team will engage with suchlike social anomalies. Hence the italicised comments below.

Many people are likely to end up living longer - and on their own. How are pupils being prepared for social possible isolation?

More jobs will be commandeered by robots. What do the educational industries teach about community cohesion? Most people will have more free time. Instead of the world of work, and the possibility of changing occupations five times or more, how are students being prepared for using their leisure time more productively?

Farms are basic for the production of food. Meat production accounts for about a seventh of current greenhouse gases. It is as if no solution to this pollution exists. But since the 1970s, anaerobic digesters have been able to help the poor to cook without choking wood smoke, thus reducing deforestation.

The EU had the power and information to have developed and distributed such technology, but failed to do so. In terms of eco-education, how long before schoolchildren learn about the pernicious tendency for politicians of all colours to bow to vested interests? Or are introduced to publications like Positive News, Green World, What Doctors Don't Tell You, and Peach News, The Ecologist etc...?

Last but not least, how can life-long learners live a fulfilling life, without knowing themselves inside out?

For us all to make a breakthrough to the other side of the stress, pain and bewilderment caused by feeling that we are a helpless victim, SELF knowledge is the most radical requirement. Thus we at ATMA give more attention to the first syllable of that word. FUN as in the word FUNction in all levels of Self development.

As for the widespread fundamental approach to academic imperatives, we give less allegiance to the last two syllables, MENTAL. There are enough mental patients already losing heart. And losing faith in the current state-run systems, just as so many victims have become disillusioned with orthodox religions as each seeks their own moral independence.

The inner ecology kept healthy needs a change of priorities and belief systems. Without ego, for Indigos in these times of strident secularity. it takes courage to be openly spiritual; especially in professions whose practitioners will not - indeed dare not - stray from the mores received in their specialist - and maybe too narrow - training.

The religious festivals of old have given way to New Age rave-ups and the like. SUPER everything is an extension of everything including the natural; and VIRTUAL reality is in another dimension to the flesh-and-blood reality most of us accept; so this human yearning is forever reaching beyond the present moment.

Those slogging away in bottom grades can aspire to Higher Education. In ending up dispirited, as teenagers they might in rave-ups want to go up - and again further UP - until a HIGH is reached. In taking a tiny pill called ecstasy I suggest these agents of artificial stimulus follow the same impulse as that experienced in religious rave-ups at religious festivals, as all reach for an out-of-body releases from the jail marked MENTAL.

When faith suggests failure like hope

How will besieged Souls learn to cope

Cleansing surrender

What might it render

You the Star role in your own Soap?

10 EDUTAINMENT?

Extra-curricula activities, like entrepreneurs starting a new venture, thrive on adrenaline. And on gallons of black coffee, silly mugs! (Made of polystyrene?) Yet ecological actions done with light-hearted love, encouraging all involved, watch personal energies rise. And why not? If it truly IS love that energies all existence, then surely the proactive love in our heart can improve personal and public prospects. For optimum energy management through a deeper Self-awareness, this is what ATMA helps to develop.

What follows now are invitations to enjoy your own bespoke lessons. The colour green plays on parts of the human psyche that craves further advancement. And that can apply to 'invisible' colours such a indigo. After all, in so-called normal terms, daydreams like night dreams can't be seen with physical eyes. Yet when feeling disconnected from the bigger pictures both seen and unseen, it's pleasing to stroll into emerald fields with wild flowers under your feet, preferably bare. Feel the carpet of soothing grass. Wander through woodlands. Perceive the cool canopies of leafy boughs above like protective arms. Listen to beautiful birdsong regaling you on your visit into their kingdom.

When RED spells danger, STOP! As with traffic-lights regulating the flow of vehicles. The colour green enhances Self-development. Permission to proceed ahead with ease? Are you in charge of your present journey with a clear notion as to your ideal destination? If not, below offers you complementary ways to refuel your relish for life with renewed exuberance and jubilations! Problematic? Maybe!

ATMA = Activating Together Monitored Activities

OLDO OLD RED EDUCATION	NEW GREEN EDUTAINMENT
12 BULLET POINTS in battery hen FACTories 4 marching cadets of consumerism into regimented classes. Uniformed orders stressed as in the Protestant Work Ethic - If doesn't hurt, it can't be doing you any good. PUPILS ARE EMPTY and IGNORANT!	**12 PULLET POINTS for hatching our own EGGZAMS based on direct experiences with life's challenges. Under our own volition is to learn how to become our own authority and personal expert. EARLY LEARNERS KNOW LOTS?**

1   VACATION - less mental stress to fear on holidays.

VOCATION - more heartfelt love to explore with all our learners.

2   IMPOSED STANDARDISATION - sold as standards.

INVITED STANDARDS - shared co-operatively.

3	LEFT-BRAIN SYSTEM-CENTRED - restricting personal choices with Humanities downgraded and the arts.	WARM-HEARTED PERSON- CENTRED- new approaches encouraging individual creativity.
4	CONFORMITY - Market driven	CREATIVE - Self-Expression
5	FUNDAMENTALISM - traditional schooling' causes the expensive Walking Wounded of education, many needing RECOVERY (Colleges?) ACADEMIES - HEAD DOWNWARD.	FUN - Philosophical PLAY the best pedagogical means to educate Soul - PLATO. Extra-curricular activities complementing State-imposed lessons can help to PREVENT mental breakdowns.

6	LITERAL rather than LATERAL INFORMATION-DRIVEN 'FACTS', MEMORY trained to replicate lessons. Paper-centred KNOWLEDGE REGURGITATION.	LATERAL before LITERAL CURIOSITY-DRIVEN to balance both brain lobes. Person-centred collegiate and HOLISTIC seeking PRACTICAL WISDOM IN ALL BENIGN HUMAN ENDEAVOURS
7	ALLOPATHIC and DEPRESSIVE, often needing remedial rescue.	EXPERIENTIAL MULTISENSORY INTERCURRICULAR.
8	OVER-PRESCRIPTIVE with CONSTRAINING RULES -EGGBOUND and EXAMBOUND - HUMPTY DUMPTY as Boss of OFSTED?	PREVENTATIVE by liberating learners from the debilitating effects of not being given enough person-centred choices. A range of complementary supports.

9	DEPENDENCY ON RULES SET BY SO-CALLED EXPERTS (adults?) OUTSIDE THE SELF WITH TOKEN CONSULTATIONS.	NEGOTIATED FAIR, FIRM BUT FLEXIBLE GUIDELINES TO ENCOURAGE INDEPENDENCE IN THOUGHT AND DEEDS.
10	PRE-PACKAGED CONVENIENCE MASS PRODUCED "MEALS" with minimal help in Self-Discovery or Self-evaluation.	CO-RESPONSIBILITY nurturing SELF-AWARENESS of real inner and outer personal needs Self-identified with guidance.

11 iTUNES: iPODs, iPADs, iPLAYER and out-of-class schoolchildren defying a system that make them feel cloned by the overuse of SELFIES as many chase unearned fame, all results of a shallow social educational environment.

Since out of schoolrooms, they treat themselves as Self-programmed home consoles in charge of most choice they make.

No wonder old-fashioned lessons do not 'click' with them any longer.

MINING ME and MINING ME2 as offered by ATMA Enterprises for inner astronauts are the first steps for travellers to mine those secret treasures hidden there within.

MY MASTER LEARNING MENU that follows, will help you polish up your best gems and to shine more brightly like the Star you truly are.

Then DOVETALES inspire a global awareness of how all aspects of life are related to you, to others and all .living.

12 'BOREDOM' is often the word used by those being led down the path to a pedant's paradise on earth.

To keep our eyes on the feet instead of the stars is to grow round-shouldered and bog-eyed. Not a healthy option for learner.

Quotes from Page 136 and others in my book, FREE SCHOOLS??? - That's the Spirit! - now on Kindle.

Enablers at ATMA Enterprises have a range of incremental Self-evaluation schemes for selected Seekers to heal the heart of their vocation in safety and to enjoy their true voice this lifetime....as never before by enjoying life's experiences.

Throughout, the true subject in ALL lessons is in all ways always YOU!

http://atmaenterprises.co.uk

THE CURATE' S EGG

'Partly *good* and partly *bad*;' without defining what the two italicised words here exactly mean, that maybe is also a loose definition of the 'the 'Curate's egg'. Even though in the present school curriculum the subject of religion - responding to the expanding interest in youngsters - has not been relegated to the Detention Room, it still contains mixed messages.

It is now some of these ambiguities I wish to highlight. But let's start with the more positive signs. Quote: 'Academias, state funded schools in England outside local authority control, have significant freedom in what they teach and do in order to follow the National Curriculum'.

In relationship to the teaching of English, Mathematics and Science, contrast the above with this quote. 'All local Authority maintained schools in England must teach these programmes of study.'

In the history lessons, blamed by some as being too 'list-like and too narrow', why not expand these by reminding students of the Crusades in the sixteenth century and the English Reformation during which the Church of England broke away from the authority of the Pope and the Roman Catholic Church. The accrued bloody karma of both of these epic events, arguably, is now being replayed, worldwide. No escape from the Curate's Egg till its 'salmonella' is cured by the consumer?

The majority of traditional school subjects have been slimmed down: less English language now giving its new emphasis on spelling and Shakespeare (even though the Bard kept changing the spelling of his name!); also, more Mathematics and Science. Why? Because all scholars, they claim, when armed with '...the essential knowledge and skills they should have...' are then more likely... 'to succeed in the real world'.

REAL? So 'They' have decided for us what IS the real world; let alone what exactly the word real really means. And without consulting you. Very clever?

This recently reappraised policy they couch within the boasted advantages of '...plus real freedom for teachers to decide how best to teach...' by giving teachers '...the freedom to shape the curriculum to to their pupils' needs'. Despite certain statutory programmes, these educational experts even invite teachers' own resources to be donated for free to the government's archive.

Playfully, I 'boasted' earlier how most of the ATMA Team of Enablers are somewhat word-blind. Dyslexic, maybe like you. When reading the previous paragraph, did you spot the deliberately included mistake? Care to look again? I'll look away now not to embarrass you!

Hint first, though. Think of a famous quote from Shakespeare whose name too often was 'misspelt'!

Well, how did you do? Probably corrected by now but I typed out exactly what I found on Google; namely '...to shape the curriculum to to their pupils' needs.' (Oh, that these too too solid words would melt into one! Seriously though, by deploying the word MUST too often, and by thus providing too many means for the self-slaughter as the ultimate in self-harm. Nearly October 2016 and it is stated on the news that overt three quarters of our young ladies have suffered from various forms of mental distress.. So much for individual autonomy. Educators, kindly become wary of misunderstanding the Star Wars' words 'May the FORCE be with you!'. Activities not honouring the individual's freewill eventually turns so septic and anti-productive, the Curate's Egg can end up addled.

Yes, the law of evolving consciousness on earth indicates that all forms of MUST will become mould. Although divine love is unconditional, even grapes on the way to become holy wine, if not treated according its their own true nature and properties, in fermenting will become musty. Consider the droves of lapsed devotees who have left the musty teachings of the over-authoritarian dogmas of the Roman Catholic Church.

Yet a similar leakage of numbers apply to the tamed doctrines of the Church of England. Have youngsters increasingly found its teachings too unstructured? If so, could it be because they have been overly conditioned to rely on the directives of 'experts', like parents, teachers, tutors, clerics, bosses and line-managers? Fortunately, some of the multiple factions sprung from Protestantism have been gaining adherents; not least the Protestant work ethic. These church services gain more arms waving noy drowning when offering more experiential ways of worshipping the Creator. Educators please take note!

Does the Curate's Egg syndrome therefore have no cure? NO! Then who better to ask than the Curate? So, does the malaise in many educational institutions have a blanket cure? NO. So, let's ask each unique student? And that, dear Indigos and other readers, is the secret essence of learning at its most fruitful; a truism which we in ATMA wish to increasingly embrace. Though it involves much work, we prefer to remain lightly playful. Especially when confronted with the darker means used to herd recalcitrant schoolchildren back into over-regulated classrooms.

Could there indeed be a FREE FAITH School, one in which all beliefs are accommodated without the owners or governors wanting to standardise mind-sets? How far away such an ideal seems from the results of Self-belief that have been warped into the belief 'I am a failure'. The damage in different forms of the 11-plus is still with us. Liz Dumbell, now at 60, is still adjusting to the debilitating effects of THEIR idea of failure from when she was eleven.

And now (at time of going to print)... God help those with an Indigo consciousness who might get sidelined once the new government, if they succeed in their intention, establish more grammar schools. If so, that surely will involve another form of the eleven-plus exam by way of selecting geochemically bright students.

Looking at the questions posed in 1944, we tried to pass the Eleven Plus as then presented (which Liz calls the Eleven Minus). We both failed it. Yippee! Many giggles as together we sought the odd word out in a list like FISHING SWIMMING CLIMBING and DROWNING. ODD indeed, if only ONE reason for ONE answer ONLY gives a pass mark. Can you spot at least THREE answers? Aiming to stay kindly and understanding (as always of course!) nonetheless we need to stay true to our insights. Hopefully, for maximum health and happiness, so do we all. How many successfully accept the challenge?

GREEN PRO FORMA

Before we offer our ideas on 'Early Inklings', a few words on 4-year-olds. Currently, their Early Stage Profile is established after their first six weeks in classes observed by trained teachers. Controversially, this is called their Base Line; that is, adults trained to toe the government's line in order to pass on this obedient mode to tomorrow's consumers. By way of a boast, those in favour will say that such a system, reducing little people to just one number by way of an educational category, is NOT subjective.

What reductionism of the human spirit. Amongst schoolchildren, no wonder knives and self-harming are alarmingly on the increase as well as an epidemic of 'sexting'. Poor dears; deprived of so much personal power in a school FACTory system, no wonder they demonstrate their private powers, as in what they each choose to do, and with whom, with hidden parts of their body.

Four densely packed pages of assessment sheets used in state schools are in green. In capital letters it is entitled TEACHER'S REPORT for ages 6-18. This approach is assembled by well-meaning educationists, a way of tackling some of the malign effects of our ailing culture.

What follows are my subjective observations on this apparently comprehensive survey of older and problematic students' character and behaviour. Seven possible boxes can be awarded a tick, though most of the multiple questions on the teacher's green pro forma provide only three options. (TWO more than in the 11 plus, so that's getting more generous!)

From this pupil survey I've cherry-picked a selection of questions. For each one I present three of my own queries. Appended to these later will be a selection of comments. Notice I did not use the word 'complaints' or 'objections'. Part of our ATMA policy is not to open boarded-up windows without permission; let alone open them wider than might be comfortable for those inside. Our complementary approach aims to avoid being confrontational but co-operatively complimentary and sensitive to prevailing circumstances.

In the pro forma, only one teacher is being consulted at a time about one child. If it was the child's mother's private assessments, or the father's, how different their child's 'scorecards' might look. That said, here are my seven selected questions under the compiler's banner title of - EDUCATION. Numbered below the banner title EDUTAINMENT, are my own querulous responses. As presented on the green pro forma, first, the compiler's questions - (not all of which carried a question-mark!)

1. How happy is he/she? (Compared to typical pupils of the same age - 7 options)

2. Hums or makes other odd noises in class.

3. Fears going to school.

4. Hears sounds and voices that aren't there.

5. Apathetic or unmotivated.

6. Feels hurt when criticised

7. Underachieving, not working up to potential.

EDUTAINMENT

1. How happy is the teacher? How Self-aware and insightful is this assessing adult; how conditioned by the current ideas about 'suitable' behaviour? Is no-one thinking of asking the child so that mutual awareness is encouraged to become Self-nurturing? Many young Indigos are with us as 'teachers' for the sake of human evolution.

2. Apart from 'Hum' being a high mantra, it resonating like the sound of bees, it might be indicating that the child is humming in order to receive more intuitions. Is not sound, as in all love-songs to God, the formative energy as ...' in the beginning was...'?

3. How many teachers fear going into school, what with the prevailing numbers of knives as students protect themselves from the consequences of a bullying system? Some folks fear hospitals. Not me. I am writing as a patient awaiting a triple bypass operation. In this cardiac ward a very frail old man has just said he was not hungry. Ignored. The kindly nurse, sounding like a trained teacher, insisted. "It will do you good, dear. You need it." Recognise those words? Education as force-feeding? We of ATMA offer MY MASTER LEARNING MENU in seven Self-selected courses. As with food, we believe that innate in each of us - even in babies who spit out

cow's milk or peanut butter - we each can recognise what we need to maximum both inner and outer growth. Wiser to acknowledge these tips and hints from youngsters?

4. Voices and visions have become anathema to professionals who assume their grasp of sanity equals their assessment of reality. In this secular society with 'patients' of all ages often aching to understand life from a higher viewpoint, mention of 'God' by their professional helpers, by contract, is outlawed. As with many practises in schoolrooms, the inner needs of students are not addressed. Worse, they are not encouraged into any Self-selected means of learning to manage themselves more effectively. Like scientific artists or artistic scientists. We collect examples of how progress was Self-propelled by those blessed ones who gave due attention to their Inner voice and their visions, as in the best of guiding dreams. Let everyone one of us feel worthy of ever better blessings.

5. Motivation, as in the self-employed, becomes more energised the more we are in charge of our formative choices. The first thing authorities who want to train us for servitude do is to limit personal responsibilities. As for teachers, that leads to a 'We know best' attitude which some schoolkids have called 'mug-'an-jug' classes, what with children already overflowing with the wish to share. Time all mugs were treated as golden chalices in need of a good daily polish!

6. The ATMA word 'Edutainment' suggests shared creative activities to serve individual and social needs. The green pro forma, as revealed above, in reeking with negativity throughout. It implies criticism of all actions and attitudes that do not conform to their very limited system of acceptable behaviour. Wisdom is never mentioned; whereas the phrase 'creative criticism' implies that cooperative kindness can prevail; that it is certainly not necessary to downgrade a growing person every time a different opinion to those being prescribed is produced. Good mental health, as with physical health, is predicated on personal Self-esteem, not enslaved by those who lack enough love and are short of empathy.

7. Since the schoolchild is hardly treated as a unique Soul, how can any adult assess this person's potential? By measuring outcomes according to the system's narrow, lop-sided, left-brain remit? Memory trained for regurgitation brings to mind the phrase, ' Sick as a parrot' - caged of course. Bow Focske has stated that 'The method for measurement in human sciences is based on a model for the natural sciences. Which takes a realist, quantifiable perspective. Yet the human experience is always relativistic and subjective in nature. So in order to fully understand the human, the study of Human Sciences would benefit from more human friendly (qualitative) methods of examination. In fact I add that all areas of society would benefit from more human friendly methods!'

Life-long education, being system-centred, can surely be improved by becoming more collegiate, one that can flourish for all concerned best; indeed, like a family when more light-hearted instead of heavy-headed.

The spirited teacher is remembered long years after their retirement. For me, it was the spirited pupils that I can still recall. Together, such free spirited folks of all ages can best experience the unforgeable joys of Edutainment.

THE HEALING HIVE

As with the Chancellor of the Exchequer, is not all-round personal happiness in all ways the cheapest social option? Many years ago, Diane Beechcroft, with others aimed to set up a consortium of assorted complementary healers. All those years back, the novel idea was that the clients were invited to meditate on their medical condition and, by tuning in, choose which therapist on offer they sensed could best address their symptoms. Since then the Rockefeller Foundation and NESTA have created a mobile-friendly DIY Toolkit (www.diytoolkit.org). It was founded to help invent, adopt and adapt ideas that can deliver better results across the board, be they educational, medical or other.

NESTA staff are collating details from an abundance of social innovations; that is, tool-kits already operating in four continents; tools that are easy to manage and navigate. They assess whether or not such practical methods in the field are not only the best so far, while others yet untried are perhaps more fit for purpose. They need to be backed up by real life case studies to show how the tool-kit under consideration has improved the life of clients. Given the financial difficulties facing the National Health Service, grass roots' health care is also included in their search for DIY strategies. This brings us back, not only to the Healing Hive but to the present researches currently being conducted in the field by Diane, as with others of us on the ATMA Team.

WAYSHOWERS AS WHISTLEBLOWERS?

Evolution, like the human need for irrational optimism, will never stay still. In India, as a guest of Brahma Kumaris, I attended an international conference of LEADERSHIP. It might have been retitled WAYSHOWERS since hand-picked, our group consisted of social, if not professional, mavericks. The course confirmed what I held to be true. That is, an astute leader takes three steps ahead of the crowd; then takes two steps backwards and waits there for the crowd to catch up. A signal from Spirit and that is the time to go forward with more like-minded Souls in service to their chosen cause.

Maybe it's now 24 years since a group of us considered setting up the Healing Hive. So it seems that the gap of time till now allowed people's consciousness to, as it were, catch up. That being so, let's further unpack some of the key words and phrases shown above in bold italics. Consider tool-kits. As current multitudes are experiencing inner guidance in practising Mindfulness, the most effective tool-kit is one's own consciousness. Hence, meditation is practical. Bespoke to purpose, it can lead us into better ways of living on purpose, inside out.

As a complete package, outer health is a reflection of our inner health. No wonder so many back-packers traipse off to India to find enlightenment. This need accepted, makes the inner workings of consciousness significantly central in all we are and from that, all we can become. India, England, Cloud Nine, the location is only an outer provision reflecting our inner requirements. However, everything we need is already within us, awaiting our best generous attention for it to manifest.

Everything being made of atoms, every conceived thing vibrates. Using inner tuning-forks, the ATMA program will pick on each incomplete 'score' and send the balancing signals in need of harmony to allow completion. The more in balance the person is the better clarity they have and the more able they are to make better assessments in all situations; but especially when it comes to their own intimate needs.

Hence ATMA' s MINING ME and MINING ME2 profiles and the seven step MY MASTER LEARNING MENU, this process altogether being inter-related, yet able to each individual's unique Self-chosen needs. Such integrated strategies can make all levels of life easier. Could we ask for more than that - and without being greedy? YES, of course! Why not ask for a deeper appreciation and acceptance of one's unique service to life?

Ready to enjoy excavating your inner treasures, secrets and best reasons for being on earth in the here-and-now? That is with

mortar-board thrown overboard as with a safely guided seafarer!

MY MISSION ON EARTH (MMOE)

THIS IS ONE OF ATMA'S SEVEN SELF-REVEALING ACTIVITIES DRAWN FROM **MY MASTER LEARNING MENU**. Abstracts given later of this as also of many other offerings from our Enablers.

Earth sustainability needs us all more than does Mars. If this approach inspires your life's mission, why not make it worth celebrating by serving societal needs more effectively? Early diagnosis is cheaper than later depression. Yet the true purpose of our gift of life at best is when usefully enjoyed in action with others. We with ATMA Enterprises are privileged to offer you so many Self-fulfilling opportunities.

Self-awareness can optimise all-round radiant health. After all, every cell of the human body 'knows' its purpose. That being so, how easy is it to accept that the whole physical organism - our body - also 'knows' what best suits its needs in order to survive. And as these facts operate at a physical levels, how much more potent must they be at the emotional and mental levels, all overseen by our Spiritual Self, knowingly? This is the golden heart of ATMA Education; one maybe best suited to those blessed if they so choose, with an amplified indigo consciousness.

Such advances give more room for Souls' needs for reliable inner messages to be heard and honoured by individuals more clearly. How clarified these were becoming when the newly formed group called ATMA Enterprises, received the news that two members needed surgical operations. I was one of them. Nothing better than to enjoy optimum good health and to experience 'illness,' as only a passing anomaly.

Impossible? Too idealistic? Beyond your capacity? Subscribe to such limiting beliefs and our unused powers shrink, if not sulk! Do you know folks who decades ago had an amazing experience, like an our-of-body trip (OOB); or a near-death encounter (NDE)? For the next forty years have they nagged the memory ragged, wondering why it only happened once? As if personal 'miracles' are rationed.

In my observation, such folks over the years allow mental doubt to seep into their Soul. The mind is inclined to accelerate this process. It seems to relish asking questions like, 'Did it REALLY happen?' 'Did I truly DESERVE such advantages?' 'Have I been DESERTED by God, and deservedly so?' Result, a self-fulfilling prophecy. Like as not, incrementally, that particular spiritual test of trust has turned into a sour disappointment.

Gratitude might have kept alive the essence of such an unforgettable experience. With that attitude, once was enough for belief to be sustained. Spirituality is not an earthly science that in all ways seeks replication. Take Bow. She is aware of this credibility gap. When visiting me in hospital, myself enjoying the prospect of a major heart operation, we shared insights.

Yes, I was a 'low risk' patient, so anxiety was not 'necessary'; and circumstances were reflecting that. In fact, I felt a fraud all through; what with no high blood pressure or temperature and no pain. To visitors I blurted, 'The best hotel - I mean, hospital, I've ever been in!"

When diagnosed, I had immediately 'known' what my future life was for. By then, even in my young eighties (Indigo age being the new sixties!) I 'knew' I was being allowed to finish off my life's work (and this book!) post treatment and with more energy. Every time the operation was postponed, I tuned into the reasons.

Surely hidden blessings were in the pipeline as in my three diseased heart vessels. My expectation - not presumption - of such blessings produced its own 'evidence'. Yes, part of my unfinished business on earth was to again link up with certain Souls in order to balance off our accumulated karma. Two nurses I then 'recognised' and eventually my faith was further rewarded. I went under the knife of the chief surgeon, a man with whom I immediately felt secure.

Throughout, I had refused to mask the pain caused by my surgical wounds despite the pressure of well-meaning medics. Pain opens up more opportunities to take charge of one's condition; not just to mask the causes for which oneself is surely responsible. After seven weeks, I ended up with four large boxes of pain killers, all unopened. They said I HAD to have them. What a waste of taxpayers' money.

Yet all ailments can be seen as a way of spring cleaning our whole system and thereby necessary for future all-round improvements. The same can be said of so-called accidents. All according to our attitudes. And some would say, 'Thanks to Cause and effect in all of our dealings, there can be no 'accidents' as such; including I might add, my own heart condition.

Eventually, I wanted to discharge myself. I was advised against it by my friend Liz Barfield. As for the District Nurse, it seems that Social Services would no longer have been available had I 'escaped' from their welfare system. Another form of implicit state 'blackmail' - or is that just another conspiracy theory, like any overblown cult, a matter of belief; no matter how we allow this to limit in so many ways the very real possibilities of better outcomes for each and all?

11 FLEXI FAITHS

Many faiths one future we hope

With less RE how do we cope

Without Higher Powers

Will Noahs need showers

If religions less cleansing than soap?

Due to council cutbacks, parents of little children were being threatened with no spaces in in over-subscribed primary schools. That prediction, potentially applying to10,000 toddlers, was made in the Spring of 2016. An official from the department of education admitted that the shortfall of parents increasingly denied their first choice of primary school was accurate; that the deficit by 2019-20 would be made up by the rapid expansion of Free Schools.

Hence, the government was keeping faith with its notion that desperate parents would set up their own Free Schools. These schools as before, would often be situated in supposedly the areas of the greatest need, including at least three northern cities.

Throughout these pages we have looked at the way that denying folks more free choices can limit, according to the 'wilfulness' of such 'victims', the full flowering of their true nature. If freewill is truly granted to all Souls, like private beliefs, such privileges can be bent by the strong character to feed their prevailing earthly needs. Though not 'greedy' for more God, think of the parents who move nearer to Faith Schools in order to get their offspring into a school with first class pass rates.

Faith Schools make up about a third of all state-funded schools in the UK. Yet two thirds of them have the right to set different admission rules, keeping their own faith system as a top priority. Yet at the end of 2015, Ofsted reported that our of 22 private Christian and Muslim schools covering nearly 2,000 pupils, nine schools were rated as inadequate. That is, inadequate as judged by the standards set by Ofsted.

Question: according to Ofsted's criteria, if there is only one way to worldly success - with hyperactive pupils on Ritalin? - how many ways are there to 'fail'? Think of the athletes who secretly take illegal performance drugs and become world famous 'winners'. Ambition backed up by conviction (not yet of the legal kind!) can become addictive; as well as attractive to less discerning fans. Society's heroes and successful monsters can seem stronger than the passive ones who feel victimised by circumstances.

These frail ones lack confidence in their personal power to change themselves for the better. So far. For Self-determination one way is to become more proactive. A universally applicable piece of practical wisdom for all ages is this: 'When the pilot is ready, the right plane appears.' In increasing numbers, that is a parent who chooses to home educate, as Sandra with her daughter Sonia.

Yet these are secular times with widening gaps between the over-wealthy and those inflicted with poverty, especially in areas of social housing. Child poverty is rife. 680,000 children in London live in substandard properties, these premises often rented accommodation. That was true of many a successful person. If you Google for celebrities who came from abject poverty, you will be amazed how lowly was the childhood of so many film stars.

Equally instructive is to note the thousands of famous personages who were born orphans with no obvious means of making their way in the world. This long list includes civic leaders, writers, artists, athletes, scientists and scholars, many of whom, like Sandra, the recovering abused orphan kid.

NEWSFLASH!

On the morning of December 29th, 2015, a new law was announced. It was to imprison up to five years anyone who has used physical or emotional coercive or controlling behaviour over another.

We read about the disabilities of learners but what about the disabilities of teachers? The mental 'torture' they are trained to inflict on little ones in the name of a consumerist society, how long before a home educator sues the Secretary of State for Education, trading on fears of failure and a one-size-fits all fundamentalism, for child abuse, under this new law?

Have you enjoyed, as I have, the company of a gypsy, an illiterate man with more streetwise wisdom than any Don I've met. Allowing the universe to be his university, without choosing to read or write, this amazing man had worked as a Self-taught tradesman in the Houses of Parliament before returning to his self-sufficient homestead where he and his family grow their own food - but SHH, probably pays no taxes. With his horses, living the life he chose, this uneducated gypsy is wiser and happier than any pedant I have ever questioned.

Not that those home-educated end up illiterate. Take this by way of an accolade for the home-schooled in America. In the mid 1990s, here is a quote from an admissions director. It read: *Boston University welcomes applications from home-schooled students. We believe students educated primarily at home possess the passion for knowledge, the independence, and self-reliance that enable them tp excel in our intellectually challenging programs of study'.*(See THE FAMILY STRIKES BACK! - a video produced by the the Meighans; that is, by Janet, the wife of the late Professor Roland Meighan, narrated by me. The copyright belongs to Educational Heretics Videos. It is part of Personalised Education Now, of which I was an early member specialising in Creativity

Across the Curriculum and that led to even long-established teachers asking me how to refresh their teaching techniques. Totally untrained in this but efforts well-received and appreciated, And I'm still at it!

The need for more Self-reliance would not be unfamiliar to most spiritual teachers. True? How many of them though, were born with a silver spoon, only to surrender their worldly wealth and rich inheritance in order to stay true to their life's mission? Like many Indigo babes these days, they seemed to have popped out of the womb oven-ready to tackle to live on the blessed message within their life's mission. Every generation has been nourished by such beacons as spiritual Wayshowers. Better still though, let's daily raise our own spirits ever higher, as if there is no other definitive way to become more bountiful, beautiful and useful.

RAISING YOUR HORIZONS

An unhappy childhood need not last a lifetime. From any life trauma, recovery is in all ways possible. And this transition can be achieved at whatever age we have been hurt deeply; confused bewilderingly; and numbed so completely that the future seems to be a fruitless as a parched desert without trees shedding dates.

Recovery needs your resilience and resourcefulness and, of course your most sincere wish to improve. You know you can. The happy heart stays open: open to opportunities; open to hope; open to higher degrees of Self-worth. In short, aim to stay open to personal optimism on all levels. At once!

But even here, with more Self-awareness, being too open can be to invite others into our life who might take advantage and sap our buoyant energies. The journey from being too 'closed up' like a hedgehog in hibernation, to being open as a mid-summer sunflower, that progress needs many kinds of help. For we who feel too unworthy to deserve help, the journey to recovery may take longer. But to take the first step is not only necessary, but brave. Yes, its takes courage to admit the need for others outside our suffering. But there is no dire situation that cannot be relieved. So seek encouragement from others and only hear positive things said in your presence. Believe you will gain unbelievable gifts and let your heartfelt belief become a magnet. Belief is your Master Key. Keep saying to yourself, 'I know I'll find the help I need'. Know it as real and, like your best dreams, it will become true.

But belief, like optimism, needs sustaining. Before determination can fade, go to Social Services or, if criminality is alleged, consult the police. In London I was mugged and in my home town, burgled. Although the property stolen was not valuable, the help I received from the voluntary Victim Support Group was exemplary.

That came to me because of the advice I received from the two caring police officers, as well as the one who checked on me a week later. Such all round help would not have been available if I had not picked up the phone and admitted I had been humiliated by strangers in my own home.

Therapists point out how many personal problems, like bad habits, keep seeming to reoccur for no reason. Yet seeking the real reason - and our own part played in these repeating patterns - is essential. Surprisingly, this is not as tough as letting a painful situation to keep on depressing us. Don't believe me, belief yourself. Believe you have the power to conquer every emotional molehill and mountain. See yourself at the peak of health, safely above all that would hurt you. For this to be sustained, changing your routine and habit patterns will help you out of any rut that makes you feel trapped.

Recovery needs you to act, you at your very best. Leave unhappiness where it belongs, in the past. Head held high look forward by helping yourself to make real your fullest potential.

Every good therapist or councillor will respond with a good heart to your willingness to openly share your dilemmas. With these new feelings of Self-responsibility and the peace of mind it brings, you'll learn how to prevent further injury as you journey with more joy towards full Self-management in charge of all your life's needs.

Better still, you might choose to help others in pain. Perhaps there is no-one better to help the injured amongst us than those who have complete empathy because they also have suffered and, at one time, seen no possibility of relief.

So spread your wings. Seek to rise above it all. As with fledglings in springtime, this needs a wish bone. Without that flexible bone linking both wings, the fledgling will fall.

So thanking your own inner wish-bone, become a high-flyer and fervently wish for full health with every bone in your body. With such sincere help and with all levels abundantly in balance, all of you comfortable with your present life's mission, that is how miracles can now happen - for you.

TRANSFORMATION

In one all boys' Inner City school, the year eight students took a year on keyboards experimenting with tunes. I had adapted my first Talking Book of New Age Family Fables into a musical. More of that in a moment.

Meanwhile, open for business...

My musical play was set in a school and with theatrical licence, reflected back to them much of their disease they already felt, albeit till then, unknowingly, about the education they were enduring. Solution, a full-length school stage show.

By way of striking a lighter note, I include now as extract from TELLING TALES. Being Fables, the original is in the genre of 'crossover fiction', often labelled YA (young adults). Below however, is the book adapted by me into a school musical. A reviewer in the local paper called the show 'magical'. Reading these lyrics, see if you can visualize this scene from Act One. It took a year, but most of the toe-tapping melodies were 'composed' by 14-year-old boys from a council house estate. On the school keyboards, they prodded different notes till reaching a sequence of notes that fitted the words and pleased the ear. Like me, not one of them knew a crotchet from a quaver. We were rescued by the Head of Music.

On stage now, visualise geography teacher Mr Cunningham dressed in drag as Miss Goodman, class teacher. As ever, she is picking on the lad's favourite friend and leader, Peter Venus. Ready, Maestro? Ready, boys? A-one, -a-two, a-three, a FOUR...

Incomplete
You perfect pest!
Just look at your sheet.
Incomplete. Peter, failed the test,
Deserves six of the best!

No marks, miss! Just bright sparks!
I've been in a dream, a globe of blue

There life is light and always new.

All your tests you've flopped
Daydreaming must be stopped.
Six of the best, six of the best
And after I gave you such a friendly warning
All nice as pie, all nice as pie

With ice-cream too, miss?

You've been in a dream, a globe of blue.

Where light is life and always new.

As the clock strikes nine next Friday morning
Your dull brain I'll awaken
Peter Venus, your buttocks must fry

My spirit must fly!

Your buttocks will fry

Like crispy bacon?

He don't look shaken!

No-one to kiss him better.
Dismiss class, double quick.
No break for you Peter, no, now hold your tongue.

We all thought we knew it all when we were young
But growing up is to learn much better
Laws have to be obeyed and to the letter.
Now at long last work and write out these lines
Knowledge is better than all vintage wines.

Dear miss, I still won't write anything down

Not till you please lose that horrible frown
Have a sweet, miss? Like to share my box?

Half empty box.
Can't sweet talk me and pull up your socks
Half empty box

It's half full too

Half empty box

It's half full too
Smarties inside
Different colour every one.
Smarties inside
Every colour under the sun.

Too old to change
I must scold for ever
Make them all clever

It's half full too

Half empty box

She'll box my ears if I box too clever

I love my class

But she can't show it

They'll only take advantage
So they can't know it.
I give them all I've got
I love not some but all the lot
Especially when they disobey
And stand in corners half the day
And cheek me when my back is turned
And leave this school with nothing learned.
I love them most of all
When I make them face the wall
Until they show respect
From my duty I'll never deflect
Nor my kids neglect
I give them all I've got
I love not some but all the lot.

Miss, the Smarties, my box had plenty
Now it's empty
You ate not some but all the lot!
And now you've lost your frown
I'll write down notes and smile.
But only for a while.

Peter, Peter Venus, so much to learn
What tall tales will help you earn?
You show no concern. I wonder why

Can't say, miss. But I'll tell you a tall tale if you like.

Oh boy Peter, on your bike!

THAT SCHOOL SOME YEARS AFTER I LEFT GOT DEMOLISHED. IT WAS DEEMED TO BE INADEQUATE. IF IT HAD STAYED A SECONDARY MODERN SCHOOL ADDRESSING THE BOYS' HANDS-ON SKILLS IN WOOD AND METAL WORK AND HOME ECONOMICS INSTEAD OF BORING THEM TO DISTRACTION WITH ENDLESS WORKSHEETS, IT AND SOME BOYS THERE MIGHT HAVE BECOME OUTSTANDING. I SAW THE POTENTIAL OF THESE YOUNGSTERS FROM THE LOCAL COUNCIL ESTATE. ONE LAD EVEN WEPT WHEN I SAID I WAS LEAVING AS HEAD OF DRAMA. RIP, ASHWORTH , ALL BOYS' SCHOOL AND OTHER SECONDARY-MODERN SCHOOLS THAT ALLOWED FOR CRAFTS LIKE WOOD AND METALWORK AS WELL AS THE IMAGINATIVE ARTS OF ALL COLOURS..

AU REVOIR

There once was a school in a shroud

Where dead ends were often allowed

So Gilmore was out on a limb like a lout

In the hope he'd be suitably cowed.

But this wily old teacher of Drama

Believed in reincarnation and karma

So he set up a spell, said 'All will be well

When Magic's the ingenious charmer!"

12 ATMA'S INVITATIONS

Mission and meaning make up ME

The template was set but Will is free

To be more in charge My life make more large

A high responsibility*!*

Even in this first year of ATMA's existence (only just, mind. I'm writing this on 31 December 2015!) Since then we have been honing gifts to share. These with your help will get further refined. You see, when working with real people in real pain and wanting to become free of their suffering, sensitivity alone won't shift those who are obstinate. Obstinacy is a form of strength, so their focus can be switched from dark to light. For everyone, hope lingers like embers in a bonfire in which Guy Fawkes did not quite die.

Allowing that everyone's unhelpful habits are reversible, here we go with synopses of our many Self-absorbing courses; all flexible enough to enable a variety of clients and a mixture of circumstances. First, as appetisers, ATMA's list of Playshops. These are offered as whole day explorations. However, for those of you to research your treasure-chest more holistically, spending half a day on any one aspects, say MY MIND, we offer the possibility that the afternoon session could become devoted to say, MY EMOTIONS. Doing all seven of the courses on MY MASTER LEARNING MENU (MMLM), your ultimate aim might be Self-Revelation. In which case, welcome. On offer now an assortment of other intriguing Playshops.

INVEST IN INTUITION & INNER GUIDANCE - with

Sue Bayley·

- Watch a small child. They know about inner guidance. They obey it in any given situation.

- As you move through your life cycles, take a minute to pause and reflect sometimes.

- Glimpse moments of clarity. When you recognise your own intuition / inner guidance, you radiate an inner knowing that no-one can dispel or deny.

- Take all of you, on a journey in this Playshop.

- *Access your own wisdom, and that of your ancestors, stored in your own DNA.

- *See what messages are revealed, as thoughts, feelings, sensations, words, pictures?

- *Share your Self-awareness with your peers in this sacred circle of confidentiality, which you co-created.

- *Take away opportunities for future investment and action.

From Through the Looking Glass by Lewis Carroll - *"Why sometimes I believed in as many as six impossible things before breakfast"*.

TRANSITION - A PALETTE OF POSSIBILITIES!

- "TRANSITION of WHAT?" you might well ask?

- *The answer to that question lies within YOU!

- *It depends on what Joys, Passions, Fears or Doubts you uncover in this Playshop!

- *And what meanings you manifest from participating in a safe setting...

- *How many times do you negate your creativity and natural gifts?

- *Take this journey, and transport yourself into a land of potential and magical possibilities. The sacred circle of confidentiality we co-create will allow you to reveal colourful and practical possibilities for you to take away and treasure.

- "Would you tell me, please, which way I ought to go from here?"
  "That depends a good deal on where you want to get to."
  "I don't much care where..."

- "Then it doesn't matter which way you go." — Lewis Carroll, Alice in Wonderland

For ATMA Enterprises, Enabled by Sue Bayley

PARENTING REVISITED – and REVISED?

With Sue Bayley and Christopher Gilmore

The more we enjoy life, the more we might like to thank our parents. And they us, their offspring. Yet resentments often linger into adulthood. Negative patterns left to fester can get passed down the generations. Tackling such blocks to achieve fully fruitful lives is what is here addressed.

Respecting every relationship as unique, Sue Bayley for years has specialised in helping Souls to see more clearly, and become more responsible, for their own gifts and blind spots.

Christopher Gilmore is also experienced in illuminating the many surprising levels of spiritual parenting; from births' blueprints to bedtime story-telling. This non-judgemental Playshop is personally tailored to the child in the adult and the adult in the child.

Warmly, we invite each participant to unpack past pains and confront current challenges; anything problematic from nightmares to the Naughty Step, all to encourage more understanding throughout the extended family.

With some Self-parenting, it is never too late to lessen the risk of future rifts. Nothing more rewarding for us than each to return to the central path some believe each personally chose, pre-birth. Even if it means using tough love, our rightful inheritance is surely best rewarded when rightful human happiness is joyfully restored.

ALL CHANGE PLEASE?

Feeling stuck at a junction? Time now to explore better avenues? All growth starts with change. Are you ready to improve your life's journey? Christopher Gilmore, your host, has run Self-improvement sessions in 4 continents and has taught all ages.

His approach to Creative Philosophy is in all ways inclusive, gentle and non-judgemental. After all, encouraging you to take more charge or your life what can become more joyful than that? By recognising the signposts and relishing the crossroads, that joy should be yours. See www.atmaenterprises.co.uk MINING ME

Attitudes can become stronger than facts. Otherwise, personal transformation could not be possible. It's in this important area of Self-development that Christopher Gilmore loves helping, having worked with all ages in four continents.

Through the years he has developed a versatile range of strategies, all aimed at folks willing to rediscover more of their dormant powers of Self-esteem.

 As an award-winning writer on personal development in a chapter called BEHIND THE CURTAIN, he sees ATMA Enterprises acting like a Healing Hive. It is never too late to harvest the honey hidden in your heart and improve your life, home and hopes. Let a better future beckon you.

See www.christophergilmore.co.uk

FROM PAGE TO STAGE −

with actor, author, playwright and poet, Christopher Gilmore

Bored at a bus-stop ever been secretly amused by the gossipers there? Or ear-wigged on a railway station a couple blaming each other for having missing their connection? Junctions are best for starting startling stories. To embellish such scenes, the first for humour; the second as drama, can be great fun as well as instructive to writers, actors and audiences. No negative critics in this supportive ATMA Playshop!

Why, because, the only experience that matters here is your own. By being alive and alert to life's wonders and to people's peculiarities, your creative energy surely wants to get your inspirations down on paper.

And then, better still, see your dialogues brought to life by yourself and/or others enacting your scenes. All to end up in a showcase for sharing with family and friends. Some of these might even recognise themselves 'on stage'!".

Christopher Gilmore on the Crewe Lyceum stage acted with Glenda Jackson and at the Edinburgh Festival with Maggie Smith. In that city, two out of thirty of his plays and musicals were presented. .He was PC Barry Clyde in DIXON OF DOCK GREEN and also appeared in EMERHENCY WARD 10 and on TV, played Prince

Florizel in Shakespeare's WINDER'S TALE. This Playshop FROM PAGE TO STAGE was last enjoyed by OAPs. But all ages welcome!

KINTSUGI (kin-soo-gee) Soul Bowls,
With Hilary Newhall

Kintsugi:"Not only is there no attempt to hide the damage, but the repair is literally illuminated… a kind of physical expression of the spirit of mushin….Mushin is often literally translated as "no mind," but carries connotations of fully existing within the moment, of non-attachment, of equanimity amid changing conditions. The vicissitudes of existence over time, to which all humans are susceptible, could not be clearer than in the breaks, the knocks, and the shattering to which ceramic ware too is subject. This poignancy or aesthetic of existence has been known in Japan as mono no aware, a compassionate sensitivity, or perhaps identification with, [things] outside oneself." — Christy Bartlett, Flickwerk: The Aesthetics of Mended Japanese Ceramics

I have developed a Playshop which involves inviting participants to consider the 'labels' they have accepted as true and which may be unhelpful and even become self-fulfilling prophecies (for example 'lazy', 'stupid', 'clumsy'). They will also be encouraged to consider themselves to have come through their experiences, embracing the Japanese philosophy behind the tradition of Kintsugi (see above). Participants will be invited to choose a pre-prepared papier maché pot from a range of shapes and colours and draw on cracks to represent some of their 'labels' which they feel are not serving them. They will then be offered the opportunity to heal those cracks with gold, copper or silver coloured foil and complete the bowl with more papier maché to create a physical, visual reminder of their 'wholeness' which they can take away from the Playshop.

LANDSCAPES? PEOPLESCAPES?
ESCAPES? LOSINGSCAPES? ...FINDINGSCAPES ~
With Hilary Newhall

"Go to the people. Live with them. Learn from them. Love them. Start with what they know. Build with what they have. But with the best leaders, when the work is done, the task accomplished, the people will say 'We have done this ourselves."– Lao Tzu

Traditional wisdom begins with the consideration of a landscape for its its potential. Findingscapes begins with people, exploring their hopes related to the provision of indoor or outdoor landscapes to ignite the Soul. A one day Playshop nvites us to explore the potential which could be met through the creation of a landscape.

In sharing examples, we'll consider and develop ideas and opportunities. Later, you will be encouraged to share and appraise each other's ideas for opportunities related to (a) specific site(s) agreed with participants. At the end of the Playshop, we will be invited to draw up a list of tasks/information required before the next session and encouraged to spend time reflecting on possibilities.

A second day, a week or more later, will provide opportunities for us to bring together information and reflections with general ideas being agreed. By the end of the second Playshop, participants will have a draft plan for action. Further Playshops are on creative designs for play and rest, using hard materials and plants, edible landscapes and landscapes for wildlife. Other Playshops available depending on the direction the first two Playshops take.

ART FOR EVERYONE, ART WITH ANYTHING ~ With Hilary Newhall

Art for Everyone Playshops were originally developed as a series of weekly Playshops (one morning a week) for Bury Art Gallery and Museums Services. The aim was to provide art materials, ideas and a non-judgmental opportunity to practice playing. The Playshops were offered to a group of low income mums with the intention that that they could then provide their children with low-cost art related activities. Feedback from the mums suggested that they were enjoying the opportunity to learn to do something creative with their children.

One, several or all of the following Playshops are offered as opportunities for adults and children to play. They are also offered in a format to encourage adults to play and pass on new ideas for creativity to children. At the beginning of each Playshop, a general introduction is given with ideas for ways to use materials.

Participants are then invited and encouraged to explore materials in their own way. Papier maché - using 'found' moulds to create unique bowls, plates etc. Printing – with a variety of 'found' and bought materials, inks and paints Playdough – cook your own!! So therapeutic, kneading warm playdough.

Explore adding colour, scent and textures Creating with scrap – don't throw that away! It's amazing what can be made with things destined for the bin rubbings – crayons, chalks, pastels – used to rub coins,

287

cardboard, wallpaper, floorboards, tree trunks …Collage – bringing ideas from the above together to create a finished piece or starting from scratch.

MOVEMENT AS MEDICINE the Nia Way –

with Patricia Mackrell

Guided by the sensation of pleasure, comfort and ease Nia takes the body, mind, emotions and spirit through a combination 52 moves, using nine different movement forms from the Martial Arts (Tai Chi, Tae Kwon Do, Aikido); the Dance Arts (Jazz, Modern and Duncan Dance) and the Healing Arts (Yoga, Alexander Technique and the work of Moshe Feldenkrais) to find your body's way of moving towards the Nia Five Sensations of Fitness: Flexibility, Agility, Mobility, Strength & Stability (FAMSS), to develop Sensory IQ.

Moving with conscious awareness using three planes of movement and three levels of intensity, Nia's routines are designed to enhance the body's ability to perform a movement with maximum efficiency and minimum effort, allowing the body to create space to naturally heal.

The Playshop begins and ends with Nia's 5-Stages of Self-Healing – an integrative movement practice based on the five stages of human development – embryonic, creeping, crawling, standing and walking.

Practiced with awareness, these stages have the power to facilitate optimal alignment, improved function and comfort in the body.

HEALING SOUNDS –

with Patricia Mackrell

Using the healing power of sound vibrations to open, clear, balance and strengthen the energetic and physical bodies this Playshop plays with the Nia "Sounding" routine using the inspiring and diverse music of Tim Wheater's "Heartland".

The focus of this routine is on establishing a connection between sound and breath as a way to enter into the world of energy where physical muscle work is replaced with a feeling of ease from using vocal sounding.

Using sound creates the grounding, the workout, and the intimacy and enhances awareness of moving your body through space. The simplicity of the moves allows for repetition whilst staying connected to the sound you make.

The body becomes the transmitter to move sound, the energy of your voice, in and out. The arm movements act as receptors, opening up to the influx of energy and allowing the thorax and throat to expand with your breath and sound.

A constant connection is made between sound and a grounded physical body. No singing is required. The mere act of listening, and then sounding your own sound, begins the process. The dynamic of the music allows for emotional vocal expression.

ENERGETICS OF NUTRITION -

Food As Medicine with

Patricia Mackrell

An introduction to the energetics of food and an understanding how food influences not only our energy levels, but effects how we feel, think, sleep and move.

Eating according to our universal needs, in that we all need food to sustain the physical body, as well as our individual needs given our age, level of activity and general health condition, we look at developing an awareness of the overall "effects" food has on us.

We look at the 7 Levels of Eating and the Wheel of Life to help us understand our cravings, addictions, habit patterns and cultural influences.

We explore how we can adopt and adapt simple and practical changes towards a more wholesome, nutritious, life-supporting relationship with food for optimum health, increased vitality and energy and to balance weight.

AN ATMA PLAYSHOP NOT TO BE MISSED. EVERYONE ENJOYS
LIFE WHEN FEELING WELL FED AND MORE HEALTHY!

SATISFIED?

My grandmother used to say, 'Always leave the table feeling you could eat a little more'. In savouring the offerings above, we hope your appetite has been sufficiently whetted for finer foods, for both inner and outer nourishment for body, mind and spirit.

Now that you've sampled our tasty menu, as with selected pizzas, our ATMA Playshops are all open to being topped up by our contributing participants. The need for personal offerings in a safe and secure setting to be trusted by all present is paramount. Indeed, consider again this quote:

'The time will come when each will be his own priest.' A mysterious and prophetic sounding oracle, one mentioned earlier, came from which holy recipe of divine dishes for discerning diners? Though it sounds biblical it came from me. Oops, sorry folks, correction. Not from me but t*hrough* me. As with everything that has or ever will exist, it all came from the epic 'Other Elsewhere'.

Thank you, dear reader, for sharing this varied feast with us all at ATMA Enterprises. If you feel that for you this could be a renewed journey of joy in action, kindly consider joining us. As social challenges continue to de-stable us, the all-round nourishment and protection of the Indigo Explorer of all Ages becomes more pressing. With our combined loving help, they can become tomorrow's leaders. We all need them. Indeed, we all need each other to improve our shared space and time. May the Blessings be ever more abundant for us all.

Other books by Christopher Gilmore

All of these wonderful books are available on Amazon and iTunes.

SOUL CENTRED EDUCATION

Help Your Higher Self Become More User-Friendly!

In this new edition of his guidebook to the Soul Plane, Christopher shows how the Higher Self is your best resource. Through "Edutainment" - or playing meaningfully - we see how all who enjoy a full life can awaken the guiding wisdom which, as Soul, we so often keep hidden. The veil can be lifted!

THE MUSHROOM MEN

Review by Keith Corbett

From World Wars to Cold Wars, Boomerangs to Swans, Christopher Gilmore draws on decades of experience as a writer and performer to deliver eloquent and thought-provoking poetry. Although published around the WWI centenary celebrations in 2014, The Mushroom Men is as timeless as it is engaging - it explores some huge topics, such as the futility of the escalation of nuclear arms, the  impact of war on our youth who face the horrors of armed conflict out of duty or force, as well as the sheer madness of death and destruction against the nature of the human Soul. His humour and hope for the future shine through.

The poems are well crafted, seamlessly blending physical world and spiritual contexts into layers of meanings that are both compelling at first blush and revealing greater depths with subsequent readings. One to revisit time and again.

ALICE IN WELFARELAND

 It's 1984 and feisty convent girl Alice falls down a rabbit-hole into a nuclear bunker - and into a world of adventures, fun and curiosity. Prejudices and the ideals of hippy Survivals are lampooned. Christopher's novel faction is inspired by the Carroll classics but rooted firmly in the nuclear New Age consciousness. 'I enjoyed reading it and happily praise it to High Heavens!' - Elspeth Cochrane, the late London Literary Agent.

His other readers unknown to him have nobbled him with comments as varied as, 'I laughed all the way throughout!' to 'I can see it being used in classrooms in about thirty years.' and finally, 'I found it terrifying!' How wonderful to collect so many contradictory reactions and author would relish.

WATCH THE BIRDIES

A Feathered Fest of Fanciful Fables!

Christopher's latest collection of family fables based around our feathered friends. As a bewitched twitcher, Christopher fantasizes on their inner lives, from the lowly sparrow to the transcendent hawk. With illustrations by Audrey Nightingale Young to colour in.

TELLING TALES

A dozen modern fables linked by the notion of the strength of goodness. The tales operate on various levels and contain nuggets of wisdom, the value of which is not always immediately apparent but tends to enrich ones thoughts in retrospect. 'Uplifting stories filled of light and laughter!' ArtsWest.

BRIGHT EYES and BUBBLES –The follow-up to Telling Tales

A second selection of family fables including *Blue Bear, The Craving Crayfish* and *Bright Eyes.* "Your stories are very interesting" Diana,10 "Funny. I like the way you don't start Once upon a time. Magnificent." Mark, 10.

Free Schools??? That's The Spirit! Vital personalised choices are at the heart of Free Schools initiatives. This book teems with well-argued and refreshingly provocative ideas appealing to all optimists who see life as our best teacher. Consider those who leave education without qualifications only subsequently to excel in the arts or business. Others with degrees stack supermarket shelves if they can get a job at all. Not an entirely new approach yet woven throughout are radical insights inviting adventurous breakthroughs...! Christopher presents scores of multi-dimensional strategies to stimulate the love of learning in all spirited individuals. By putting a happy heart before a hurting head this book places students of all ages at the centre of their own learning choices.

<u>DOVETALES</u> – 10 illustrated books

360+ Creative Inter-Curricular Insights and Activities covering 10 subjects, each in a dedicated volume. Questions as stimuli – for your answers!

Arts Within   Fewer Tears, Finer Fears?

Godly Geography Less Green Gloom, More Mother Love?

Holistic History   Fewer Disasters, More Déjà vu?

Integrated Science Love Before Learning?

Loving Languages More Babel, Less   Babble?

Mighty Mathematics   More Fun, Less Fear?

Musical Meditations   Octaves of Awareness?

Religious Experience   Dreams With The Supreme?

Sports, Health & Dance More Grace, More Uplift?

Technology for All   Fewer Boxes, Further Bridges?

Praise for Dovetales:

"Brilliant" Ashley, 10, on Dovetales Technology for All - Fewer Boxes, Further Bridges.

"Each mini-saga lasts a whole lesson. Things that you wouldn't think of, but it all fits in." Lee, 15, illustrator of Mighty Mathematics, More Fun, Less Fear.

"Innovative, should be an integral part of every school library"

R. Rendall, Deputy Headteacher

"Fascinating and Inspiring. Gives hope for the future" Anna Craft, Open University

"A golden treasure-chest overflowing with innovation…beyond the limits of the National Curriculum, full of endless innovation." Bonnie Alexander-Hill for the journal CADUCEUS, Healing into Wholeness

SUSALL PLAYSHOPS AVAILABLE -

With **Christopher Gilmore**

SEEKERS UNITING SPIRITUALLY ALL LOVING LEARNING

~

INDIGO EDUCATION FOR SPIRITED LEARNERS

~

(L)EARNING FROM PAST LIVES?

Déjà vu etc & Loving Links!

~

LOOKING 4 YOUR HIGHEST SELF

On message & mission?

~

(L)EARNING WITH ANGELS

Messengers who help us

~

SACRED SECRETS, HEALING SOUNDS

At-tone-ment and at-one-ment

~

INVISIBLE POWERS IN YOU ALL

Spirit V Tech?

~

MANY MINDS AT PLAY

Multiple Intelligences?

~

HOW KIND IS KOSMIC KARMA?

Cause & Effect?

~

CREATIVE PHILOSOPHY, THE MAKING OF ME

Mapping the journey more accurately

~

LOOKING-GLASS ALICE & TODAY'S AGELESS INDIGOS?

~

DREAMS AND ASTRAL ASTRONAUTS

Sleep's multiple riddled lessons

~

ALL CHANGE PLEASE

Repairing my Spiritual Profile

~

THE AQUARIAN GOSPEL of JESUS the CHRIST,

PEACE through INTER-FAITH

~

TEACHINGS ON NON VIOLENCE

~

RELIGIONS, ROBOTS AND RABBITS

Occult puzzles?

DISCOVERING ATLANTIS – IN YOU

"Wow – awesome Guy!" Comment by 'Darkangel' following broadcast on Atlantis

~

SINGING UP THE CHAKRAS – Experiential scales

~

UNEXPECTED ANGLES ON ASTROLOGY

~

SOUL-CENTRED EDUCATION

Completing Karma

~

BRAIN-GYM AND ENERGY MANAGEMENT

~

MEDITATION AS MEDICINE

DIY Divinity

~

CREATIVE PHILOSOPHY

Cradle to Grave and Beyond

~

MY IDENTITY AUDIT

The Making of a Better Me

~

SPIRITUAL HISTORY

Through 7 Rays and Multiple Cycles

COSMIC CLASSROOMS

Inter-dimensional Intentions

SACRED FABLES

with Winged Creatures,Unicorns and Totem   Animals

~

DISHONEST TO GOD

disentangling politics from religion?

~

DEATH AS A SWING DOOR?

~

ATMA DOVETAILS

Creativity with Cosmic Consciousness

FROM PAGE TO STAGE

Acting out our conflicts

I have facilitated spiritual 'Playshops' in 4 continents & welcome invitations! See www.christophergilmore.co.uk

email:christopher_gilmore@ymail.com

Mob: 07837971408.

Find me on Facebook: christopher.gilmore37

YouTube: www.youtube.com/user/Christophergilmore?
feature=mhee

CONTACTS WORTH EXPLORING?

Radiant Living – patricia_mackrell@hotmail.co.uk

ADHD Lancashire – bee@adhalancashire.co.uk

Peace is Possible – graham.pedley@yahoo.co.uk

Trafficlights4peace – TL4peace@hotmail,com

Vision OM – vision-om@gmail.com

Sacred Geometry – matthewdonnelly82@hmail.com

Personalised Education Now (PEN) – 900 440 0115 925 7261

The Findhorn Foundation - https//www.findhorn.org

Education Otherwise – www.education-othewrwise.org

Hypnosis for Change – hypnosis4change30@yahoo.uk

Academy 4 Empowerment – keith@academy4empowerment.com

Access Consciousness – be@thewellworls.co.uk

NORTHWEST SPIRITUAL EXPERIENCES GROUP -
-info@meetup.com

@llchange – Hilary.at@change.co.uk

Sacred Geometry – matthewdonnelly82@gmail.com

Womens Network – lady2704@gmail.com

Teacher Support Network – phone 020 2697 2750

Squeaky The Clown – info@squeakytheclown.co.uk

Tibetan Prananadi Massage – Email – contact@lotus-san.ro

Counselling psychotherapy – jcsmith@therapy-cheshire.co.uk

John Harrison author of The World in your Hands – www.john-harrison-palmistry.com

Robin Guilliard – Crewe Graphics – rob-guilliard@hotmail.com

Co-editors, Richard House Self & Society – richardhouse@hotmail.com

Green Spirit – info@greenspirit.org.uk

humphreys peter personalisededucationnow@blueyonder.co.uk
www.theoceancleanup.com
Campaigning Community Avaaz meaning Voice https://avaaz.org
https://goodcountry.org/
http://interspirituality.com/
https://data.org/FAQ
https://www.contemplativemind.org/programs/acmhe

https://communityoflovinaction.org/
www.presencing.com
www.nesta.org.uk
http://economicsandpeace.org
www.sharing.org
www.alternatives.org.uk
www.xchange.iofc.org
www.innovatemyschool.com/magazine

london@lucistrust.org